I0795579

ADVANCE PRAISE FOR *RAY KHAN*

"With *Ray Khan,* Lou Valoze joins the ranks of great autobiographical law enforcement storytellers. And what a story he has to tell, from harrowing undercover ops to the deeply complicated relationship with his star confidential informant, the amazing, confounding Ray Khan. Together these two—against seemingly impossible odds—become an unstoppable duo, removing innumerable crime guns from circulation and thwarting organized criminals at every turn. Told with humor, gut-wrenching drama, and just an all-around flare for great crime stories, Lou Valoze and his co-writer Kerry Linfoot bring a story to the page that readers (and very likely viewers as well!) will be enthralled with for many years to come."

—Matthew Carnahan, writer
and creator, *House of Lies*

RAY KHAN

THE BETRAYAL OF AN INFORMANT

LOU VALOZE
AND KERRY LINFOOT

Post Hill Press

A POST HILL PRESS BOOK
ISBN: 979-8-89565-390-6
ISBN (eBook): 979-8-89565-391-3

Cover design by Jim Villaflores

This is a work of nonfiction. All people, locations, events, and situations are portrayed to the best of the author's memory and knowledge. Although adequate research was undergone concerning criminal cases, real-life people and perceptions, and authentic situations and incidents, the author and publisher do not assume and hereby disclaim any liability concerning any legal or criminal details present in this book. While all of the events described are true, many names and identifying details have been changed to protect the privacy of the people involved.

Post Hill Press
New York • Nashville
posthillpress.com

Published in the United States of America
1 2 3 4 5 6 7 8 9 10

CHAPTER ONE

Ray Khan's job description was simple: Go out on the streets and create relationships with the most violent criminals out there. Make friends with the people putting illegal guns on the streets, the people poisoning communities with dangerous drugs, and the trigger-pullers sticking guns in people's faces. Once you've accomplished that, tell them all about your associates who are willing to buy these illegal guns and drugs so they can resell them to make a profit. Convince those people to come to your place of business to meet and engage in criminal activity. That is what Bureau of Alcohol, Tobacco and Firearms, and Explosive (ATF) Agent Lou Valoze told Ray he needed to do. In exchange the ATF would help Ray stay in the United States legally and defer the bullshit federal cigarette charges Ray faced. Simple.

So, Ray started working for Agent Valoze as a confidential informant. Over time, Ray had proven himself to be the most effective informant Valoze ever used, but Ray wasn't there for the takedown of his first undercover operation. He was in state custody and once again facing deportation proceedings, thanks to an obsessed and overzealous state revenue agent named Billy Thompson. Once again, Valoze managed to prevent Ray from being deported so he could help with the next undercover operation in Savannah, Georgia. This operation proved to be one of the most successful undercover operations in ATF history. There would be two stages to this operation, and each would require two separate takedowns. Ray Khan was not only present for both of these takedowns, he was the star of the show.

ATF was asking a lot of Ray Khan. Specifically, for the first arrest operation resulting from Operation Crossbones, Agent Valoze was asking a lot. This operation lasted for nearly a year, and the agents hadn't dealt with many of these criminal defendants for several months. At this point, getting them all to show up on the same day was going to be an extremely difficult task. Agent Valoze needed Ray to bring them all to the undercover warehouse, at very specific times, on the day of the arrest operation. And all these defendants, without exception, were unreliable, erratic, and violent. It was the reason why ATF management decided these criminals needed to be arrested early in the operation. They were still out on the streets committing violent crimes and putting illegal weapons in the hands of other criminals, and ATF obviously couldn't let this continue with their knowledge.

Agent Valoze had a plan. The defendants needed to be arrested as quietly as possible. The second phase of the operation was moving to a different location, but the ATF needed to wall off these defendants and keep their arrests quiet. This takedown needed to be executed flawlessly. If any of the other ongoing targets heard about it, the second phase of the operation was doomed. And it was all on Ray's shoulders. In preparation, Ray had recently gone to two of the defendants' places of business to purchase small quantities of drugs, which solidified the probable cause needed for search warrants of those locations. While there, he saw guns in plain view at both places. Basically, the entire operation hinged on Ray Khan doing what he does best: bringing bad guys into the undercover law-enforcement world.

The arrest operation or "takedown" of a long-term undercover operation is a daunting task under any conditions. For this first takedown of the undercover operation in Thunderbolt, Georgia, ATF had to include numerous agencies: the US Marshals Service, ICE, the Savannah Police Department, and the Chatham County Sheriff's Office. Keeping things quiet with all those agencies involved was going to be difficult on another level. Much the same as the undercover portion of this operation, the takedown had to be covert.

It wouldn't be Agent Valoze and his team of undercovers out in the warehouse greeting defendants when they arrived. That would be all Ray. The agents would be watching from the safety of an adjacent room as Ray met the defendants and lured them inside. Ray was to bring them inside the warehouse where agents staged a truck container the defendants believed to be full of brand-new televisions, DVD players, and stereo systems. The electronics were the bait, and Ray was holding the fishing pole. But when Ray opened the container doors to show the defendants the televisions, ATF Special Response Team (SRT) agents would be waiting inside to descend on them and take them into custody.

In preparation for this takedown, federal indictments had been granted for all these defendants. Most of the charges involved firearms and narcotics trafficking. All of them had lengthy criminal histories and some had previously been deported from the United States. Every one of these defendants had been introduced to Valoze and his undercover crew by Ray Khan. How was this person able to gain the trust of some of the most violent criminals on America's streets? Ray had never used drugs. He knew absolutely nothing about firearms. He was not from the streets. If you ask him about it, Ray will just smile and shake his head. But more about that later. For now, we will go back to the arrests.

To lure these defendants into the warehouse one last time, Ray Khan told them he had a truck full of stolen electronics arriving that day. He told them he would sell the devices dirt cheap if they showed up right after the truck arrived. Ray was instructed to stagger the defendants' arrivals throughout the day so ATF could arrest them cleanly. The US Marshals would then whisk each arrestee away before anyone else saw them, and Ray would set up for the next defendant's arrival.

The Southeast ATF Special Response Team, an elite unit composed of agents from all over the region, the Marshals, and the Savannah Police Department, would conduct the arrests and secure any associates the defendants brought with them. Ray arranged the arrival times so none of them would get spooked by seeing law enforcement when they pulled up. He told them to park in the back, as they usually did, and enter through the bay doors. The agents parked a huge container in one of the large bays at the back of the building. The container, which was supposedly filled with the stolen electronics, would, in reality, be full of tactical officers, armed to the teeth and ready to pounce on the defendants. The entire undercover warehouse had been set up as a trap to catch the targets and anyone else who showed up with them. Over the past year, Ray and the undercover agents had been able to make the targets of the operation comfortable enough to show up to the warehouse and conduct their criminal activities. The hope now was that they would be comfortable enough to show up to the warehouse one last time to get a great deal on some stolen DVD players and televisions.

Everything relied on Ray's timing and his ability to quickly draw each defendant into the warehouse. He was the focal point of this entire takedown. Ray was also the main reason the undercover operation succeeded. He was the one who had cultivated relationships with these defendants. He had brought them to the location, introduced them to Agent Valoze and his team, and started the ball rolling so undercover agents could purchase guns and drugs from them. It all centered on Ray—and this was just the way he liked it.

At this point in their time working together, Ray had shown Agent Valoze time and again that he had no fear. Ray always wanted to be part of the action and, more importantly, he was loyal to a fault. He had been instrumental in making Valoze's last case one of the most successful long-term undercover investigations in ATF history. Now he was playing a major role in making this operation even bigger and better.

As with every high-risk takedown conducted by ATF, the leader of the ATF SRT team developed a takedown plan. Only this time, the plan needed to include an excited and proud Ray Khan. The day before, the members of this highly trained unit began conducting rehearsals of the arrests. Agent Valoze and the undercover team played the role of the defendants with Ray Khan playing himself. As the teams drilled through the rehearsals, it became almost comical as Ray, who had no tactical training or experience, started directing traffic and telling the SRT guys how to do their jobs. At first, the team leader seemed to be getting a kick out of it, but eventually he pulled Agent Valoze aside.

"What the fuck is this guy's deal—is he your informant or is he a fucking ATF supervisor?" he asked.

"Just let him do his thing, brother," was Agent Valoze's response. Laughing, they continued rehearsing.

Ray was responsible for communicating and coordinating with all the defendants to make sure they showed up exactly when planned. This was done through phone calls and text messages right up to the moments before they arrived. Trying to get criminals of any ilk to show up on time is notoriously difficult. Scheduling them for their own arrests just added to the tension.

Ray arranged for the first defendant's arrival early that morning. All the law enforcement officers involved in this takedown had been separated into teams which were stationed strategically inside and outside of the warehouse. Everyone knew their assignments once the defendants started to arrive. There were even chase teams located nearby and a helicopter in the air. Ray was positioned at the bay door behind the warehouse, pacing back and forth and making last-minute phone calls to defendants.

The first target scheduled was an extremely violent convicted felon who had sold numerous guns to Agent Valoze. His name was Diego, a primarily Spanish-speaking guy who had been previously deported and had an arrest warrant for armed robbery. Diego called Agent Valoze to let him know that he was close by. Less than a minute later, he pulled up to the back of the warehouse, parked his car, and walked up to the back door. Ray greeted Diego at the door, shaking his hand and leading him inside the warehouse. As Ray guided him to the door at the end of the container, Diego was asking Ray about the televisions Agent Valoze had described and which were supposedly in the container.

At that point, the doors on the back of the container flew open, and a sea of SRT members in green tactical uniforms aimed their guns at both men. As he had been instructed, Ray hit the ground. As he dropped, however, he saw Diego reach for a gun in his waistband. Before he could even get a grip on his gun, he was pelted with less-lethal rounds. It was hard to tell which sound was louder: the sound of the beanbags hitting his chest or the sound of his body smacking into the concrete floor next to Ray. Diego somehow got to his feet and foolishly decided to make a run for it, but there was nowhere for him to go. He was immediately tackled and handcuffed by SRT members who restrained, zip-tied, and searched every defendant with brutal efficiency. As it turned out, Diego also had a gun on his ankle, which flew out when he was tackled to the ground. This was not overly surprising as he was a previously convicted felon. As soon as he was in handcuffs, his vehicle was quickly searched, resulting in the seizure of several large bags of cocaine and two more firearms. Both the defendant and his vehicle were transported to a prearranged processing area. Not a bad start to the day.

The next defendant to arrive was one of the most unpredictable and violent criminals the undercover team had dealt with during the entire operation. Dale sold guns and drugs to the undercover team, but almost every transaction came close to ending in a fist fight. He was a hulking, aggressive guy with a bad temper and a short fuse. He arrived shortly after Diego and his associate had been transported, but Dale brought another person with him, presumably to help him load all the electronic equipment they were going to acquire into their vehicle. Ray greeted them as they got out of the truck and brought them both inside. Once again, as Ray guided them to the container doors, they were in for the surprise of their life. The doors flew open, and they were surrounded by men in green shouting commands and pointing guns at them. Ray ducked for cover, but instinct kicked in for Dale and his associate and they both tried to run. Within seconds, both men were beanbagged while trying to escape, and both were knocked off their feet. The man who accompanied Dale was stung with multiple beanbag rounds, and he splattered on the floor, lying there motionless. As they handcuffed and searched them, the SRT agents realized this man had defecated on himself, soiling both his jeans and the large bag of crack cocaine in his back pocket.

As the day went on, every last defendant Ray escorted into the warehouse either attempted to run or tried to fight, and all of them felt the consequences. Some were chased and bitten by police dogs, others were tased or felt the painful impact of less-lethal rounds from SRT firearms. Not every law enforcement takedown has this much action, but this was a direct result of the violent nature of the defendants Ray Khan had introduced.

One of the most notorious defendants that Ray cultivated in the entire operation showed up that afternoon, and all the undercover agents knew this guy, Karl, was not going to be taken into custody without incident. During the undercover firearms transactions with the agents, he acted extremely difficult and unpredictable. Negotiating with him on prices had been nearly impossible. In every transaction, Karl had demanded totally unrealistic prices for the weapons he was selling. Prices so high that had the agents actually paid them, not only would they have lost all street credibility, but they would have left themselves open to an entrapment defense. During these price negotiations, Karl would fly off the handle, yell and scream, and had even gotten in Agent Valoze's face on several occasions—and Valoze is not a small man himself. When Karl showed up for the takedown operation, Valoze and his team were all secretly hoping for him to act up and get thumped by the SRT. They were not disappointed.

Karl, along with two members of his crew, showed up at his allotted time in the afternoon, expecting to receive a bunch of stolen electronics at a bargain price. Undercover agents watched the monitor as Ray greeted him and escorted Karl and his crew members towards the container. As Ray brought them closer, the door flew open and the guys in green were there to greet them. Immediately, Karl heroically shoved one of his crew members towards the awaiting SRT agents and took off. Out of nowhere came Ray Khan, running right behind him. The SRT guys were unable to shoot Karl with their beanbag rounds because Ray was in the way. Unbelievably, Ray was able to catch Karl from behind and take him to the ground. The SRT members were on him instantly to get Karl restrained.

The undercover agents watched this entire scene unfold from the monitor room. Agent Valoze couldn't help but be proud of his unlikely confidential informant, who had now interjected himself into the tactical arrest of an ATF defendant. Ray had done the unexpected—the impossible, even. But this was nothing new.

Each of the defendants who showed up that day were greeted in similar fashion, and each reacted in the same way. While Ray didn't tackle anyone else to the ground, his ability to execute the difficult, intricate plan to perfection was nothing less than remarkable. None of the agents, tactical team, or law enforcement personnel were injured, and it was all due to Ray Khan.

***

Most normal people couldn't imagine finding themselves in Ray's situation. If you talk to Ray, he understands his life isn't normal. I mean, how many federal informants do you know? How many of them walk free, confident, and willing to put their stories and real names into a book like this? It'll soon become clear that Ray is cut from a different cloth than most other people. Ray's story is strange, certainly, but it's one hell of a ride.

This is the story of Ray Khan, arguably one of the most successful informants ever used by the federal government—and his betrayal by the very agencies he served.

CHAPTER TWO

If you ask Ray about the time he was arrested by ATF, he'll stick to a single story: "One of my employees was stealing a pack of cigarettes a day from my stores. I got them for her."

He'll insist he didn't buy the untaxed cigarettes for resale, and you won't change his story, no matter how many times you ask. ATF Agent Lou Valoze asserts that Ray knew exactly what he was doing. He was buying untaxed cigarettes to sell in his gas stations. Whoever you choose to believe, Ray's choice unexpectedly initiated a long and fruitful partnership: special agent and informant.

When asked about Ray Khan's career as an informant, former ATF agent Tom Lesnak says, "What sets Ray apart from any other CI I've worked with is, most CIs have a lane. Ray is the only guy I've ever worked with…he didn't have a lane. I could drop him and ask him to go into any single criminal world, and he would do it."

What Lesnak is telling us here is that ATF typically brought in specific CIs, or confidential informants, for specific cases. The

CI needed to know the illegal business they were infiltrating. It also helped to match them, whether experientially, ethnically, or otherwise, to the targets. It kept them safe and maximized their effectiveness in their role. This wasn't the case for Ray Khan. Black, white, Hispanic, bikers, street gangs, or money launderers: Ray brought them all in. And he still does it to this day. "Ray Khan" is not his real name, of course, but it's the one that resonates within federal law enforcement agencies to this day. However, we are getting ahead of ourselves. The creation of Ray Khan started a long time before he'd ever met Lesnak, or Ray's primary handler, ATF agent Lou Valoze.

Ray's path to becoming a federal informant was atypical. He was never involved in gangs, guns, or drugs. Born in Ahmedabad, the largest city in Gujarat, western India, Ray intended to follow in his father's footsteps and become an officer in the Indian Police Service. Due to his father's esteemed rank as an associate commissioner and his forty years of service, Ray grew up around law enforcement and saw the prestige, the firearms (which are otherwise rare in India), the drivers, and the big houses they were awarded. He also took notice of the respect these officers received. These were benefits Ray coveted, his eye already on nice rewards in exchange for hard work. However, his father's job meant they moved around a lot, sometimes up to four times a year. It made Ray good at speaking to people and making new friends, but it didn't help his education. He took the notoriously difficult police entrance exam on multiple occasions, but Ray couldn't pass, despite going to New Delhi to participate in concentrated study for the test. Thousands of people take this exam every year, but only a few hundred achieve the grades necessary to progress past the test.

"Very hard exam," Ray says. His Indian accent is strong, and the unexpected emphasis on certain words can be off-putting to many Americans. It sounds bossy, insistent, and borderline rude to most native English speakers. Once your ear tunes to the cadence, however, Ray's speech style becomes part of his personality. It's different—but somehow intriguing. Much like the man himself. "Maybe pass first or second phase," Ray explains, "but third phase you cannot pass. That test was very tricky. You have to take so much practice with this test."

Ray's unexpectedly playful personality comes through then as he confesses the third phase of the exam required preparation and repetition. It required writing specific answers in a strict time crunch, sometimes as little as twenty seconds. But Ray freely admits now that he had been spending time with his girlfriend instead of practicing.

"Now I can pass it," he says, his typical confidence in himself and his abilities shining as strongly as his accent.

But this confidence was hard earned. Over the past twenty years, Ray has wiped out multiple times. He's been jailed, detained in ICE facilities, and he's come out penniless. Repeatedly. Now he's a multimillionaire with a Rolls-Royce worth over $600,000. So how does a failed Indian police recruit end up in America, living his best life? It wasn't an easy road, but it's one which eventually made his father proud.

At the age of twenty-two, after failing the police entrance exam for the third time, Ray fell back on his master's degree in chemical engineering and opened his own company buying, transporting, and storing industrial chemicals. While creating this business, Ray married his high school sweetheart in India, but all her family lived in the United States. She gained US citizenship through her family, so she was often away. Ray's son,

Kamal, was born in America in 1996, but it was 2001 before Ray first visited. A family trip to Chicago changed his life and his priorities. Ray had experienced American life, and he wanted more.

He'll play it cool if you ask him, of course. It's the Ray Khan way. "No, I just came for the green card," he says, not betraying even a touch of excitement. Ultimately, however, his decisions about that green card would have far-reaching repercussions—more than he ever could have known.

Over the next few years, his chemical company booming, Ray spent as much time as he could in America. He began the green card process with sponsorship from his wife, and all was going well until Ray was arrested for domestic violence by the Hanover Park Police Department in Illinois.

"It did not happen, anything. Nothing has happened. She was boiling the eggs, and the eggs explode, and she had burn on the face. And that morning my sister told the police, 'Oh, he beat her,' and my wife didn't say anything, so the police took me in the jail. But next day my wife came to the judge in the court by herself and told the judge her face was burning because of the eggs."

Ray's story is likely one faced by many immigrants. He was scared and couldn't defend himself to the police. "I tried to tell the police, but they didn't listen to me," he says. While his wife's sister spoke English fluently, Ray was talking with his wife in Gujarati but couldn't explain in English what had happened to the police. Fortunately for Ray, his wife was in the witness box the next day, and she told the judge everything.

While he was trying to sleep on the stone bench in jail that night, Ray's mind raced. He didn't know he'd be freed the next day, but he decided he needed a change regardless. Living with his wife's family was becoming increasingly difficult. The arguments were increasing in intensity, and Ray knew he couldn't trust his sister anymore, not after what she'd told the police to get him arrested. He didn't know why his sister would say such a thing, but he suspected it was something to do with her husband, Nital Patel. Remember this name. It will show up often in Ray's story.

Once he was released from the DuPage County Jail, Ray made the first move of many. Relying initially on money from his Indian company, Ray left his wife and started over. He first started work for a temporary labor service and impressed his manager so much that he got hired right away.

"HR hired me and give me Honeywell badge and everything," Ray tells me. He goes on to say, however, that there was "too much snow every day, so I use all those [holiday] days and told them one day I can't come no more and I quit the job. I don't like it. Those were good people, but I was not liking working for someone else. In order for me to start my business I had to quit my job first."

After working for a few companies in the quality control field, Ray grew more and more tired of listening to other people. He hated the weather in Chicago and knew buying a business there would be more than he could afford. He was also used to being his own boss. So, Ray made the decision to leave Illinois, and he bought his first gas station in Statesboro, Georgia. Unbeknownst to him, the ATF had also set up shop in the same small city.

Known historically for its role in race-related violence in the decades following the civil war, Statesboro, the home of Georgia Southern University, is now a picturesque town of forty thousand people in eastern Georgia. There were half as many people there when Ray relocated in 2006, and the low-income, working-class environment offered Ray the chance to get his foot in the door with a fairly inexpensive investment.

Ray bought a gas station for $40,000 using a loan from a local bank—apparently, they didn't need to check his citizenship status. Luck like that follows Ray Khan around. What might seem like insurmountable odds to normal people are things Ray takes in his stride.

"At that time bank was so easy. They were good people, good people. So, I found one gas station, so they were asking like forty, fifty thousand dollars for gas station. So, I went to the bank, and I am asking that bank manager guy for fifty-thousand-dollar loan. That time Marty was the main manager. He was talking to me all the time. And he said, 'For what?' and I said, 'For this gas station and for ten thousand dollars to put in my bank account so I can run it.' And he said 'OK, come tomorrow, twelve o'clock.'"

Unfortunately, when Ray arrived the next day, Marty wasn't there. Resolved to wait for him to return, Ray approached his assistant and asked how long it would be.

"Mr. Khan?" she asked. When Ray identified himself, the bank manager's assistant handed him some paperwork to sign. She then handed him a check for $50,000. And just like that, Ray Khan became a US business owner.

It wasn't easy. At first, he worked all the store hours himself: 6:00 AM to 11:00 PM, seven days a week. But Ray was no stranger to hard work. He created a successful chemical company in India and he now applied the same work ethic to his store. He was almost out of cash at this point, and the loan was a huge risk. If this business failed, Ray would be broke, illegal, and completely alone. But it will quickly become apparent that Ray Khan is not afraid of a little risk.

As Ray tells it: "Then I worked morning to night by myself. No employees. I needed to pay off this loan first so I'm just working by myself. Just kept working over there."

For fourteen months, Ray kept up this punishing schedule. Running on little sleep and his natural charisma, Ray's business slowly began to turn the smallest profit. He spoke some heavily accented English, but Ray has a surprisingly effective way of connecting with people. His upbringing makes him naturally deferential, respectful to his customers, but anyone who knows Indian people understands any maintained politeness must be earned. It also doesn't extend to everyone.

He was working alone one night, as he always did, when a man entered his store. "I knew he wasn't the ordinary customer," Ray says. "He was strung out. Dirty."

Leaving his storeroom, Ray walked back to his counter. If this man was dangerous, he wanted a barrier between them. He had no weapons, but a bat would have come in handy. Using his cameras and the mirrors positioned strategically around his store, Ray watched the man pretending to look at items on the shelves. After a couple of minutes of walking around the store to build up his nerve, he pulled out a gun as soon as he stopped in front of Ray.

"Give me all your cash. And the cigarettes," the guy demanded, his hand shaking as he held the gun at Ray's chest.

Other than seeing his father's service weapon, and those carried by Indian Police Service officers who visited his parents' home, Ray had no experience with firearms. The gun pointed at him was silver. That's all he can tell you. He doesn't know the difference between a semi-automatic and a revolver, but he knew there was a gun aimed right at his heart. His options were limited: Give the man what he demanded—or act. Ray Khan chose the second option. He hadn't worked all these hours over the past few months to have this drugged-out punk walk into his business and steal from him. Reaching across the counter with a speed surprising for such an unassuming man, Ray grabbed the gunman's arm and stripped him of the weapon. Again, surprising his assailant, Ray leaped across the counter, leaned back, and slapped the man right across the face.

Here's the story in Ray's own words: "Like one time when I was working over there about nine, nine thirty, one black guy came over there to my counter and asked, 'How much money you got? Give me the money.' And I was just looking at him. So I just grabbed his hand with the gun and slapped him four, five, ten times and took his gun and slap, slap, slap, and just tell him, get out from here, and he was like 'sorry, sorry, sorry.'"

Chased by Ray in his agitated state, the man left with haste. Ray never saw him again. When asked whether he reported the incident, Ray will look at you like you're crazy. It didn't even occur to him.

"I'm thinking he is stupid. Why did this guy come in front of me? That time he comes and does like that. I all the time saw big guns at the house with the police, and my dad had guns at the house. AK-47s and all that, and lot of police around my house all the time," Ray says. He goes on to say, though, "Statesboro is the small town, I did not want any attention. He doesn't know who I am and how I am in India. I tell him, get out of here and don't come back. And tell all your gang never come here. They never try to rob my gas station again." He then simply threw the guy's gun away in a plastic bag.

"I didn't want to call the police, and I didn't know if what I did was wrong or right, and I didn't want no kind of attention from anyone." It's then that Ray's good heart shows, just for a brief moment. "I don't want that guy to be in jail, either. He just has kids. Maybe he was my customer."

For his own immigration and business-based reasons, Ray dealt with the incident himself, and considered it handled to his own satisfaction.

Around this time, following more conflict with his wife and, more frequently, with her family, Ray's wife withdrew her support for his visa application. Her family kept calling him and claiming Ray only stayed married to her to keep his green card. In response, Ray contacted US Citizenship and Immigration Services and returned his green card. He then made the choice to remain in the country illegally.

"That was my big mistake.... Otherwise in 2003, or something, I would be citizen," Ray shakes his head as he says this, probably imagining how things might have been different. "When I was young, at that time I have so much proud, self-respect [pride]—that's why I give away the green card that time." His decision was made, though, and by the time 2007 rolled around, Ray found himself trapped. He couldn't leave the United States, or he risked not being able to return to his son or his fledgling business.

It's hard work, but the convenience-store trade can be profitable. As long as the overheads are managed and the supplies are selected to create maximum revenue, there's a great deal of money to be made. Ray's risk and hard work were paying off. Around 2008, he finally hired an employee for the Statesboro store, and then leased his second convenience store an hour away in Vidalia. Ray's empire was underway, but not everyone was happy about Ray's success.

Ray has two sisters; one lives in the United States with her husband, Nital Patel—there's that name again. When Ray immigrated, being closer to his sister was an added bonus. Although some distance had grown between them since she married, Ray loved his sisters, and their father trusted him to watch out for them. When she married Nital, Ray believed his sister's care now fell to her husband. Nital's version of love, however, was isolating and cruel. He shielded his wife from her family and saw Ray as a threat. He slowly poisoned his wife against her brother, eventually leading to the false domestic violence charges which landed Ray in jail and Ray's surrender of his green card application. None of this was known to Ray until he contacted Nital for advice after buying his first gas station.

"Nital knew the business," Ray says, "But he is not so good at it."

Nital had some financial troubles, but he had been in the convenience-store business for several years. Ray thought he might bridge the gap which was widening in his family, and he tried to speak to Nital about business ideas.

"He told me to get lost," Ray confides. Nital refused to help Ray, but as Ray found success through his hard work and natural shrewdness, Nital's bitterness grew. Though he was unaware of it at the time, Nital's jealousy would create some dire consequences for Ray.

By April 2009, things seemed to be going well for Ray. His second store was much easier to manage, now that he had experience. He hired a manager for that location and checked in with them daily. He hated losing control, but even the great Ray Khan couldn't figure out how to be in two places at once. As he wasn't spending all the hours of the day at his stores, Ray now had more time for himself and more time to socialize.

Ray noticed the head shop on his way to the gym each day—at least that's what he'll tell you. Most who know Ray would be surprised if he'd ever spent much time in a gym, but that is Ray's story, so we'll go with it. Each day he'd drive by, waving from his Cadillac Escalade to the guys smoking in front of the head shop,

Smokin' Sal's II. The newly purchased car was Ray's pride and joy, and he didn't mind drawing attention to himself as he drove it around the small town.

On one of these alleged trips to the "gym," Ray decided to stop and talk with the workers at Smokin' Sal's. He caught the odd glimpse inside the building, and what he saw intrigued him: cigarettes by the caseload. Ray's no fool. This wasn't a licensed tobacco distribution center, but Ray was always on the lookout for cheaper goods for his stores. Though the men outside the store were very different from him—big American gangster types—he saw an opportunity. Strapping the Ray Khan courage to his back, he approached the business.

The store owner who stood and greeted Ray should have intimidated him. Well over six feet tall, heavily muscled, and covered in tattoos, the man looked like he could be the bouncer in a dive bar or the enforcer for an outlaw motorcycle gang. He towered over Ray's 5'9" frame—his glaring presence not particularly inviting for someone working in the retail industry. Ray took it in stride. Strolling forward with his hand out, he introduced himself. Whereas others might have turned and left, Ray's instinct for trouble, and the possibility of making a quick buck, propelled him forward.

"Sal," the big guy gave his own name. "Sal Nunziato."

Ray knew he was onto something as Sal slowly warmed to him, bringing him inside the shop. Ray told Sal he owned several convenience stores, and Sal's eyes widened ever so slightly as Ray wandered around the head shop. Glass pipes and lighters filled shelves under the counters, but it was the displays on the wall that drew Ray's gaze. Cartons and cartons of cigarettes, one of Ray's most profitable but expensive items, were piled high. And Ray could tell these cartons weren't stamped.

The taxing of cigarettes in Georgia, as in most states, is controlled by the Department of Revenue (DOR). Typically, tobacco wholesalers receive bulk shipments from a manufacturer and then assess the appropriate state tax, which is set by DOR. A physical "stamp" is then affixed to the product to indicate relevant taxes have been paid. The Georgia tax rates vary between 7 and 25 percent, or an average of approximately forty cents for each pack of cigarettes.

"These cigarettes don't have the Georgia stamp on it. You don't sell it like that. You will have trouble. You sell these cigarettes?" Ray asked, not knowing this question would change the course of his life.

What Ray saw while talking to Sal was a way to increase the profits in his stores. What Ray didn't see was that this head shop was actually an undercover ATF operation, and "Sal" was actually ATF Agent Lou Valoze. While these operations were not targeting cigarette trafficking, what Agent Valoze saw was the potential seizure of a brand-new Cadillac. What nobody saw at this time was the beginning of an incredible partnership.

Telling "Sal" he was buying the cigarettes to give to an employee who was stealing a pack a day from his stores, Ray bought twenty-six cartons of untaxed cigarettes during that first meeting. When he came back two days later, Ray bought a master case: twelve thousand cigarettes for $900, saving more than $200 by avoiding the taxes. His story about giving the cigarettes to an employee was thinning by the carton.

"I'm taking a trip to New York soon," Ray told the agents when he ordered four more master cases, or forty-eight thousand cigarettes. When he left the store that first day with his twelve thousand cigarettes and put them into his new Cadillac, Ray was unaware he committed a federal crime.

According to the ATF's Contraband Cigarette Trafficking Act (CCTA), it is "a federal crime to ship, transport, receive, possess, sell, distribute or purchase more than 10,000 cigarettes without tax stamps in the states which require tax stamps".[1] According to the CCTA, even one untaxed cigarette over ten thousand is considered a significant quantity, thereby falling under the category of "contraband." From the perspective of the ATF, the trafficking of untaxed cigarettes is often an indicator of more serious criminal activity, specifically money laundering and the financing of narcotics and weapons trafficking. Agent Valoze calls CCTA-related charges "chickenshit," but what he saw that day was far from it. By placing the twelve thousand cigarettes into the Cadillac, the vehicle became what is known as a "conveyance," and thus was eligible for seizure.

Over the next couple of weeks, Ray returned to Sal's and bought five more master cases of cigarettes. He then asked to purchase all the Mores and Camels in the store. To shore up Ray's charges, Agent Valoze again told him they weren't tax stamped and even showed him where the stamps should be.

"Yes, sir. I see that," Ray told the undercover agent, nonetheless agreeing to pay $4,500 for the master cases. He also bought twenty cartons of Camels for a further one hundred dollars.

"And I need more Newports," Ray said. "As soon as possible." This time he let it slip that the cigarettes were for his convenience store in Statesboro. ATF had him.

When they closed the undercover head shop operation at the end of April 2009, ATF planned to indict Ray alongside a

---

1 Bureau of Alcohol, Tobacco, Firearms and Explosives. "Contraband Cigarette Trafficking Act." *ATF Bureau of Alcohol, Tobacco, Firearms and Explosives.* Last updated September 28, 2022. https://www.atf.gov/alcohol-tobacco/contraband-cigarette-trafficking-act. Accessed August 10, 2025.

host of narcotics and firearms traffickers. When his name was entered into the system, Ray's illegal status in the US was also flagged. By May 2009, however, Ray was also facing charges from the Bulloch County Sheriff's Office for having a gambling machine in his Statesboro store. These state charges were Commercial Gambling and Keeping a Gambling Place. Ray was arrested on these state charges, taken to jail, and held without bond due to his Immigration and Customs Enforcement (ICE) hold. After a few days in jail, an immigration judge granted Ray permission to voluntarily depart the United States, and his ICE hold was released.

What Ray didn't know was that his brother-in-law had been influential in his arrest. For reasons unknown to Ray, Nital had contacted a friend, Georgia Department of Revenue agent Billy Thompson, and informed him of the unlicensed slot machine in Ray's store. Although this was not a serious crime, Nital's influence led to Ray's arrest and possible deportation. And his brother-in-law wasn't done with him yet.

Despite his immigration woes and the state gambling charges, Ray bonded out of Bulloch County jail in late May feeling optimistic, as only Ray Khan can. He knew he would find a way forward. Just as he'd done when he left Illinois, Ray made a conscious decision to keep his head down and remain in the United States illegally. He was facing some major legal issues, but no one could have predicted how everything was about to change.

On June 24, 2009, Ray was arrested on federal tobacco-trafficking charges, and his brand-new Cadillac Escalade was seized by ATF.

"I was working in the morning and there's a lot of police," Ray says. "I thought, 'Something happen outside maybe.' I thought, 'Is something like a robbery happen? Or something [else] happen?' So when a lot of police come, I just go out and say, 'Why? Why? Why?' And then they say, 'Oh, this is ICE.' I say, 'What does it mean, ICE?' I don't know anything about them back then. He just say, 'I need your ID.' I give it to them, they ask, 'You have paper?' I ask, 'What kind of paper?' They say, 'Green card, or something?' I say, 'I used to have, but I give it to you back.'"

Ray was taken to jail in Statesboro, and from there directly placed into a carrier and sent to an ICE holding facility in Atlanta. His arrest canceled the first ICE judge's order permitting him to voluntarily leave the country just a few months prior, in part due to the fact that Ray hadn't left. Despite Ray's optimism, it seemed his run at the American Dream was about to come to an end...until Ray's lawyer approached Agent Valoze.

"My client will be the best informant you've ever had," the attorney told Valoze. "He just wants to stay in the country."

"Well...," Agent Valoze considered. "I can always use another informant."

As Agent Valoze and Ray Khan tell it, "Ray was not even a thought in this operation. We had a hundred defendants. They were all gangbangers, drug dealers, but because he was illegal, he was kind of fucked. So, they weren't even going to prosecute him for that, but his lawyer, an Indian guy in Savannah, he was not a good lawyer, by the way..."

"He took my money and everything. [The ICE agent] said, 'I see in my computer you used to have green card.' But I tell him I give it back. 'So you are illegal and I can book you.' And after a few days, four days, five, six days, they took me to the immigration judge and he say, 'OK, you don't have nothing at all.' I said, 'That's fine, Judge,' and I request the judge, 'I have my son, he is very small. At least let me voluntary departure. I can go to India, and I can provide my passport right away. I can provide my ticket, and you can put me on the plane with my son. So, I can go back to India.' And judge grant my voluntary departure."

Once again, Ray was given leave to exit the country on his own terms. What Ray didn't understand at this time was that this agreement to voluntarily depart the US would forever show up on his immigration record in big red letters as "DEPORTATION" , a brand which would haunt him for years. Or, as Agent Valoze so articulately says, "It's like herpes. It never leaves your life."

"What happened was, because he was illegal, they charged him with the cigarette violations," Agent Valoze continues. "So his lawyer came to me and he said, 'Listen, if you can help my client out, he will work for you, and he'll be the best informant you ever had.' I said, [Valoze looks at Ray] 'No offense to you, Ray, but what can this guy do? I deal with gangbangers. He's got no history of violence, guns, drugs, and he doesn't know that world.' I didn't even really want to, but I thought, I'll take a chance on this guy. I liked how he carried himself."

Valoze says he asked the US Attorney's Office for permission to use Ray as an informant, and they agreed. Ray had received another reprieve—and a chance to stay in the country legally.

"I didn't really expect much from him. I mean, what can he do? It's going to be more of a pain in the ass for me, and now I have to be his babysitter, and if he fucks up it's all on me. So Ray and I sat down, and I told him, 'We're going to start this new undercover operation in South Georgia, specifically Glynn County.' Ray and I talked, and I told him the concept, and what we'd be doing. We would be selling cigarettes, but the main goal was to get crime guns and dangerous drugs off the street. I told him, 'The undercover agents don't leave the store. You will be our guy on the outside and bring the criminals to us.'"

"I said, 'Make me the owner.'" Ray recalls his response to Valoze's proposed operation. "You guys work with me, and they will believe me. So, most gas station people, are mostly Indian people. If that's the way, people will believe me, and I go the bad areas and handed over the cigarettes and all kind of stuff to the people and talking to all kind of bullshit outside, guns and drugs, and I bring everyone to the undercover store."

It was then that Valoze and his new informant came up with his new name: "Ray Khan." Valoze kind of loved the play on words of "Khan" and "con," and at that moment, Ray's life changed.

Operation Statesboro Blues closed just days after Ray came in. Had he waited just a little longer before contacting the agents at Smokin' Sal's, his whole life would have been different. But Agent Valoze's mind was on his next project: another long-term undercover operation which would become one of the most successful ATF ever conducted, ironically in large part due to Ray Khan's involvement.

CHAPTER THREE

With the support of the US Attorney's Office, with whom Agent Valoze maintained a close relationship based on the success of his first two undercover operations, the ATF requested a stay on the ICE procedures against Ray Khan. He was eventually granted "deferred prosecution" and permitted to remain in the US, as long as he adhered to certain conditions. The main condition was that he needed to be useful to the ATF and their new operation, code-named Operation Ceasefire.

Located now in Brunswick, Georgia, Agent Valoze's new investigation aimed to target specific violent groups and gangs plaguing the small community. The statistics of gun-related violence and narcotics crimes far exceeded what should be expected in a small city, and the Glynn County Police Department (GCPD) were outnumbered and out of their depth. Methamphetamine was flooding their previously tranquil streets, and the associated gang violence was depleting their meager resources. There was also a significant home-invasion crew working repeated jobs in the area, and the local cops had no idea how to combat these unpredictable attacks. They needed to think outside the box, and they needed help.

During a post-operational briefing for the operation in Statesboro, Agent Valoze was approached by a high-ranking GCPD officer, who requested assistance in their community. Mere months later, ATF had their next long-term undercover operation, only this time it came with a risky add-on bonus. The add-on was one the ATF was not quite sold on. This time, the fictitious business would be a military surplus store with an attached three-lane shooting range.

Obviously, the July 2009 proposal for this idea was met with strong initial resistance from ATF Headquarters. It was bad enough that violent criminals would be bringing weapons into the store to sell. Now they were going to be allowed to shoot them, too? It was difficult for Valoze to sell. To add insult to injury, when the proposal reached one member of Valoze's ATF chain of command, it was denied with the reason, "It just doesn't feel right."

Valoze was pissed. What kind of reasoning was that? How could he make this idea "feel" better?

It took some negotiation, and a bit of tact and finesse, which was not his strong suit at that time, but Agent Valoze's proposal eventually won out. ATF realized that, by requiring inspections of firearms before they could be used on the range, their agents could collect information on more weapons than those being sold to them. They could also identify a wider range of people illegally in possession of these guns. Despite their concerns for the agents' safety, and with strict surveillance systems in place, the project was green-lit, and Operation Ceasefire began.

Initially funded through a grant from Project Safe Neighborhoods, the cover company, "Thunderbolt Surplus," was set up in Ray Khan's name, according to his request. Agent Valoze was listed as the business's manager, and other federal and local law enforcement officers were listed as employees. As a result of the support from the US Attorney's Office, and despite resistance from the Georgia Department of Revenue, the gambling-related state charges against Ray had been dropped. Suddenly, Ray found himself legally in the country and no longer facing any court proceedings. Needless to say, his gratitude towards Agent Valoze was boundless. Known to him from this point as "Lou Sir," Agent Valoze and his team became Ray's priority. Ray had a clearly defined moral compass when it came to drugs and violence. The only problem was how to make contact with the criminal element in a town he did not live in and where he didn't really know anyone. As far as the agents were concerned, that was Ray's problem. They had little investment in him at this point, and if he didn't work out, the support offered through Ray's confidential-informant agreement could be easily withdrawn. As former agent Tom Lesnak will tell you, this agreement is for the benefit of ATF. It offers no protection to the CI.

By this time, Agent Valoze and his team had become resourceful when conducting these operations. ATF is small when compared to most other three-letter agencies, and it is also relatively underfunded. There was no big pool of money to draw from when setting up and maintaining these large operations. The involved agents had, however, previously made contacts with former law enforcement officers who offered important resources. These enterprising former cops set up businesses that stored huge amounts of counterfeit merchandise seized by law enforcement agencies throughout the country. The sheer bulk of this evidence took up warehouse-sized hangars, and police departments had no room to store it in their evidence vaults while their cases were being adjudicated. These hangars stored the items for them, and once the case was over, the businesses would dispose of the counterfeit merchandise. Sometimes they were able to donate items to law enforcement agencies, like ATF, to be used as props in undercover investigations. For this reason, it was with a trunk full of fake jeans and jerseys, pirated DVDs, counterfeit electronics, and, of course, unstamped cigarettes, that Ray took to the streets.

Ray will tell you he chose lower socio-economic neighborhoods in the area and simply walked up to people sitting on their dilapidated doorsteps, in weed-ridden apartment parking lots, or in trailer parks. He reasoned that this was where gun and drug crimes were mainly being committed. He rolled into these areas in his new Cadillac Escalade, the previous one having been seized by the ATF and now being driven, rather cruelly, by Agent Valoze. But Ray didn't mind. He even joked about it with the undercover team. These neighborhoods, however, housed Spanish-speaking illegal aliens, younger black males being drawn into gang life, and hardened white biker-type guys, with whom Ray had nothing in common.

Imagine this: you speak broken English. You know nothing about guns. Or drugs, or crime, really. Now the ATF asks you to go into these neighborhoods you would prefer to avoid at all costs. You aren't a fighter. You're a businessman. You must approach dangerous criminals, people in gangs, and drug dealers. Murderers. No shit, they would eye you with suspicion when you approached.

"Who the fuck is this guy? Who does he think he is?"

Groups of young men. Gangbangers. Bikers. Criminal organizations. People so different from Ray that he had no way to connect. How would you manage this mammoth task you need to accomplish to stay in the country, near your family?

Ray did it using his swagger. His balls. He strode into these groups, these gatherings of dangerous people, using arrogance as a shield. His motivation for walking up to these gang members and engaging with them, should you ask him, was to keep firearms and narcotics away from schools. There was also that little ICE motivator, but Ray will cleanly skim right past that. He'd walk right up to big groups of criminals, flashing his counterfeit-clothing stock and handing out bootlegged DVDs. Over time, they'd just accept his presence. It truly was a thing of beauty.

"I just went into the bad neighborhoods. I never use guns or drugs, but I'm not scared of those things. I told you about that guy in my store," Ray reminds us.

Ray put counterfeit Nike sneakers and fake purses inside his car and then he would "go to the bad areas," Ray says. There, he would "see the people outside, talking to them, give them the stuff for free." Ray explains that, when he would visit for the second or third time, people he met would give him their names and welcome him into their conversations.

Ray would tell them he was the owner of the store. "They believe that because Indian people have everywhere gas stations and all, so they believe that." As the conversations progressed, Ray dropped the information that he had shady people working for him and he came from India to make money. "Just talking all kinds of stuff. I talk to them all the time. When I am talking to the bad guys and I'm telling them like I'm doing all this bad stuff. I just say we're getting in all kinds of stuff and doing bad things. I just lie all the time."

"You need something?" they would ask him, and only then would Ray say they needed guns to resell in New York. "And I was there talking to all kind of these people, and I just hand it [counterfeit merchandise] out to them and just tell them to come down to the store. Like I go to the bad neighborhood and all people sitting outside, so I sit with them outside and talking to them, and talking about the guns and drugs too, because my guys like good stuff but we are having trouble getting it. And they say, 'We can bring it,' and I would then just tell them [the agents] who is bringing the guns or cocaine to the store."

Once these basic introductions and guidelines were set, the people Ray met would come and check out the business, unaware that it was actually an undercover ATF operation. Then they would come back again. With guns. And then they would just keep coming. Ray would tell them that the more guns and drugs they could buy and then resell for a profit, the more cheap cigarettes they could get for the store.

"I always act like I am a bad guy too. All these people they become friends with me." Ray makes it sound so simple. Yet, his motivations remained clear and firmly rooted in his father's law-enforcement background. "But even with those guns and drugs, I think my kids go to the school, too, and those people might give it to them. So, I feel like I can do what I can so those kids don't get those guns or drugs."

Agent Valoze says that once Ray made the introductions, the undercover agents wanted Ray out of the picture so he didn't have to testify should any of these cases end up going to court. So, Ray Khan just drove his fancy car around Brunswick, introducing himself and handing out DVDs of pirated pornography, untaxed cigarettes, and counterfeit purses or clothing. Then he would slowly turn the conversation away from drumming up business for his newly established surplus store to the business of guns and drugs. Easy, right? To Ray, there is nothing easier. His frequent moves due to his father's job meant he was used to speaking to strangers. When you are moved to a new school every few months, you become accustomed to making friends quickly, and Ray excels in this area.

"First time he calls me," Valoze remembers, "about this white tweaker guy with a gun. The guy comes in the next day with the lowest form of a gun (a .22 caliber Marlin rifle); turned out to be stolen and he was a felon—a violent felon with an armed robbery conviction. And that's how it started and it just fucking spiraled. Next thing I knew Ray's calling me saying, 'I'm sending in this guy with crack cocaine, then another guy with meth, then someone selling ecstasy.' And then pretty soon these guys are selling me grocery bags full of ecstasy, tens of thousands of pills. He would send these guys in, walking with a 'pimp limp,' and they'd get up to the counter and pull an AK-47–style rifle out of their baggy jeans."

Ray also spent time with other Indian store owners in the area, chatting and drinking tea in their stores, and he was beginning to create a network of street-level contacts. As the gangbangers came in to buy their "loosies" (single cigarettes), Ray talked to them. When patched bikers rolled through to gas up their Harleys, Ray approached them. Whenever any lowlife the average person would avoid showed their face in the stores, Ray was there to chat. Under his disguise as the owner of a military surplus store, he'd slip them a couple of Disney DVDs for their kids, or a fake purse for their girlfriends. He'd tell them this was a sample of what he was selling in his store, and then he'd mention the shooting range. Many of these characters wouldn't go to the respectable gun ranges, what with the strict rules and the law-enforcement presence, but Ray's place was different.

Next thing the agents knew, Ray was "in the know" in South Georgia. He came to know the local gangs, home invasion crews, drug dealers, and guys selling guns on the streets. He created his own network, and it spiderwebbed.

"Slowly, slowly we learn like lot of stuff and that's how slowly, slowly we get like bigger people, too," Ray says. He'd bring interested parties into the store, introduce them to the agents, and the agents would take over. It didn't take long for Agent Valoze and his team to realize that Ray was a natural. Soon, the agents were buying large quantities of guns and drugs from people Ray was bringing in.

"I know about cocaine 'cause I'm watching the movie, like *Scarface*, but I don't know what is the ecstasy or anything," Ray recalls. "One guy, he pull bag out and I say, 'What is that shit, man?' And he say, 'It's ecstasy. You don't need it?' So, I called Lou Sir, "You need ecstasy, or not?' He said, 'Yes. Tell him to bring it.' I say, 'Come on, man. Follow me." Next thing Agent Valoze knew, this guy was in the store with a shopping bag full of different colored pills and a federal narcotics distribution charge in his future.

"Ray never wore a wire, and ATF controlled the venue," Valoze says. While some people would try to sell Ray the guns when he visited them, he always said they needed to bring the guns to Sal, Valoze's undercover persona. The bad guys had to come to the agents, which removed most entrapment issues. But it also left Ray alone in the field, with no backup, no radio, and no rescue teams. "Ray's conversations and his methods and techniques were never put under scrutiny. How he got people to the store was unknown," Valoze says. And it didn't take long before Ray was bringing in some seriously bad people.

The main area of the undercover operation had large car bays, accessible through big bay doors. One day, Ray brought in this raggedy-looking biker dude, who definitely had a past. This worn-out looking older white guy, who introduced himself, no shit, as "Cowboy," asked if he could rent one of the bays in the store for his car-repair business. Having played this game before, the agents knew that someone like Cowboy, who was well known in the criminal community, could bring in more people like him and, therefore, broaden their operation. A few weeks after Cowboy set up his "car-repair business," the warehouses were raided by the Glynn County Police Department because he was in fact running a chop shop with stolen vehicles. But that is another story.

At this point in his career, Agent Valoze had an absolutely clean file, which was very rare for someone who was always assigned to the streets and had worked undercover for as long as he had.

"You have to act like you are just as bad as the bad guys that you are dealing with, you know," Valoze says. "So that's why you cannot go straight by the book or follow all your agencies' policies and procedures. So, if you are on the road out there in the field, you cannot call your boss and ask for permission to do something or ask if your actions are within ATF policy. By that time, some guy's going to kill you for your indecisiveness."

When recounting his next story, Valoze likes to think back to a legendary ATF undercover agent, Jay Dobyns, who he worked with on a few undercover operations. Jay spent two full years undercover with the outlaw Hells Angels Motorcycle Club (MC). When asked about needing to break the rules during his time with the MC, Dobyns is reported to have said that undercover ATF agents would take the law seriously. But they would consider ATF policies and procedures as mere suggestions. ATF Agent Valoze took this to heart.

Despite this outlook, however, Valoze never even had an accusation of any improprieties in his entire law enforcement career. As Dobyns implies regarding his own work, this was certainly not because Valoze never violated any of ATF's policies and procedures; it was because, whenever he did violate them, it was for the right reasons, and his supervisors stood by his decisions. Valoze's view of his own actions was about to change, however, when Ray brought Cowboy into the undercover operation and he told Valoze that one of his associates had a PKM machine gun he was trying to unload.

The PKM is an extremely durable and reliable machine gun and has been used to kill a lot of people around the world. Not only did Agent Valoze really want to get that gun off the streets, but he also knew any associate of Cowboy's had to be a real scumbag. Cowboy would become one of the most bizarre defendants of Valoze's entire career. He looked a little bit like the actor Sam Elliot, but not as cool. He was usually in the company of young black drug dealers, who all seemed to respect him. He had already introduced many future defendants in this operation, even referring to a couple of them as his sons. Some of these youngsters ended up selling undercover agents thousands of ecstasy pills during the operation. Cowboy, who was also a convicted felon, had already sold Agent Valoze a number of guns, including AR-15 and AK-47 rifles.

At this point, Cowboy had proved himself to be enough of a high-level player that Agent Valoze knew he wasn't bullshitting about the machine gun. Valoze told him to tell his friend to bring the gun in, but Cowboy said there was no way his friend would do that. Agent Valoze told Cowboy to bring the gun to him, and he could "broker" the deal. This is when Cowboy said his friend would want at least half of the money up front, and the price was $6,000, non-negotiable. Despite Agent Valoze's attempts to convince Cowboy he should trust him at this point and he shouldn't have to front any money, Cowboy said his friend didn't trust anybody as he'd already been to prison several times.

In a decision which would come to haunt him, Agent Valoze decided not to write a report about these conversations. It was all just words at this point, right? A lot of guys came into the operation and talked a lot of shit about things they could do, and nothing ever came of it. If they wrote reports on everything, the agents would never get anything else done. So Valoze asked Cowboy if he could at least produce a picture of the gun, with him in it for authenticity's sake. About a week later, Cowboy came into the business and showed the agents a picture on his phone. It sure as hell was a PKM machine gun, and Cowboy's tattooed hand was on the stock.

"The golden rule of undercover work is you never front the money," said Chris Bayless, Agent Valoze's mentor. It was also ATF policy. And for good reasons. For the most part, if you give money to a criminal in exchange for the promise of him delivering contraband, you will never see your money or that criminal again. ATF made this a policy after numerous agents had been burned fronting money over the years. In Agent Valoze's mind, however, there were always exceptions to the rules, and he felt like this was one of those times. The purpose of this operation was to make the community safer by removing dangerous weapons from the streets, and the PKM was one of the most dangerous firearms out there. Without telling his supervisor, so he wasn't part of the act, Valoze made the decision and fronted Cowboy the $3,000 from funds brought in from the warehouse sales.

Normally, Agent Valoze would have had a team of agents follow Cowboy to see where he went to get the gun, but because he was doing this "unofficially," that wasn't an option. He was confident Cowboy would quickly return with the machine gun to get the rest of the money. His plan was to record the transaction when he returned and write it up then. When it got to be about closing time, though, Agent Valoze was getting a little concerned. They closed up shop, and on the drive back to the undercover house Valoze called Cowboy and got voice mail. Repeatedly.

The next day, it was business as usual. A couple of gun buys, a few dope deals, and it was about an hour before closing and Agent Valoze still hadn't heard from Cowboy. "Never front the money." His mentor's advice rolled through his head hour after hour. Valoze's partner, Sonny, knew he was doing a slow burn, but none of the other undercovers or the cover team knew what was going on.

About thirty minutes before closing time, Agent Valoze told Sonny they were taking a ride after they closed. The agents had a good address for Cowboy from his file, and he was on probation, so they knew he was staying there. When they got there in Ray's Escalade at about 10:00 PM, Cowboy's van was parked out front and there were lights on in the house. Agent Valoze parked on the street and told Sonny to go around back as he approached the front door. He knocked loudly and, when a female called out, he said, "It's Sal, and I need to talk to Cowboy right now."

"He's not here," was her reply.

About this time, Agent Valoze heard a commotion out back. He ran around the house to find Sonny had Cowboy on the ground in a headlock while he was mashing his face into the dirt. "Where the fuck were you going?" Sonny was yelling at him.

Valoze moved Sonny off him, rolled Cowboy over, and kneeled on his chest. By this time his wife had come out and was screaming that she was going to call the police. Sonny was shouting back at her, "Do it, call the fucking police," while Cowboy was also screaming at her to not call anyone. Valoze knew he needed to do this quickly and get the fuck out of there before the neighbors really did call someone.

Holding the older and much smaller man down, Valoze told Cowboy he was going to break his arm if he didn't return the money right then. Cowboy swore he had already given the money to his friend and said he was picking up the gun in the morning because he didn't want to bring it back to his house. If Valoze really was a gangster, he says he would have snapped his fucking arm right then and made Cowboy ride with him to his friend's house to retrieve the money or the gun. But he wasn't a gangster. He was a federal agent, and he was already on shaky ground. Agent Valoze let Cowboy off the ground and pinned him against the back wall of his house, reminding him that he and Sonny knew where he lived. If they didn't have either the money or the gun by 1:00 PM the next day, they'd be back.

As Sonny and Agent Valoze headed back to the car, Cowboy yelled out, "Sal, can I ask you one question?"

Agent Valoze snapped around. "How the fuck did you know where I live?" Cowboy asked.

"You think I'm gonna hand three thousand dollars to a motherfucker without knowing where he puts his head at night?" Valoze responded. There was no way "Sal" should have known where Cowboy lived, of course, and Valoze's response was quick thinking. They just had to hope Cowboy bought it.

He did.

About fifteen minutes after the store opened the next day, Cowboy pulled into the parking lot in his van. The agents watched him remove a large duffel bag from the back and bring it into the store. He placed it down on the counter and smiled. "Here you go, Sal." Agent Valoze unzipped the bag and took out a pristine PKM machine gun.

After looking the gun over, he handed Cowboy $3,000 in official government funds for the machine gun. Cowboy bullshitted with the agents in the warehouse for a few minutes, as if nothing had occurred the night before. For a seasoned gangster like Cowboy, what happened was just business. Then he walked out the door. That was the last transaction that they would conduct with Cowboy.

When his boss heard about that deal, he called Agent Valoze to congratulate him. He was a gun stroke (a term ATF agents use to describe firearms aficionados), and it wasn't often that they were able to buy a gun like that off the streets—even with Ray's help. "That's a great price for that gun too. It must be stolen," his boss said. Agent Valoze will tell you he felt bad for not telling him the whole story. He still does to this day. But he couldn't. Never make your boss part of the conspiracy.

Cowboy successfully finished his state probation during the timeline of Operation Ceasefire. When he was arrested on the ATF charges in the takedown, he was given an elevated high bond by the federal judge. Despite this, he was still one of the few defendants who managed to post bond and go home pending his trial or plea agreement. ATF then received information that, while he was out on bond, he was still selling narcotics. The agents were able to insert a female undercover, through an informant, who bought drugs from him. He was immediately re-arrested by the US Marshals and ended up receiving one of the biggest sentences in Operation Ceasefire. As a result, Cowboy will probably die in prison. These were the types of people Ray was dealing with—on both sides of the warehouse counter.

As the undercover operation gathered steam, Ray was bringing in more and more bad guys, who were selling as many guns and drugs as the operation could buy.

"At one point, we had to turn away a bunch of cocaine," Valoze confesses. "We just didn't have the money to buy it."

As the agents became busier, they recognized they needed help sometimes and they started bringing in assistance from other ATF agents around the country. This was required when Ray brought in two young black kids about ten months into the investigation. One of the selling factors when Valoze proposed Ceasefire was that the investigation would target a home-invasion crew who were operating in and around Glynn County. As the months passed, however, the agents heard nothing about those involved—until Ray brought in those two young men. When they started speaking with the young gang members, the agents quickly realized Ray had inadvertently hit the home-invasion jackpot.

"I had so much stuff going on by that time, there was no way I could help with that part of the case," Valoze says. Fortunately, though, he knew someone else who specialized in these types of investigations, and he called up a fellow agent who was working in Miami. They had to wait a few months until the operation was coming to a close to avoid blowing the whole Brunswick investigation. It was a gamble, but the agents decided the takedown of the home-invasion crew had to be done in conjunction with the takedown of the entire warehouse operation. Finally, when the time came, Valoze introduced two of the Miami undercovers to the crew, and his Florida partners arranged their own takedown.

"The Miami guys set them up with a stash house to hit. You need to get the conversation going, right? Need to get them to show up in their gear, weapons loaded," Valoze says. "It was a phenomenal case."

The ATF was initially resistant to the staged home invasion. They worried about a bunch of armed guys showing up to a takedown. The US Attorney's Office was concerned. Their worries, however, centered on the optics of operations of this type, which seemed almost racially motivated, as they only targeted groups of young black men. Despite these concerns, however, the takedown went without a hitch.

"These are the kinds of people that Ray brought in," Valoze says, shaking his head in wonder even years after the operation had ended. "It was just Ray Fucking Khan doing what Ray Fucking Khan does."

How did Ray keep his nerve when dealing with these dangerous people? You might ask. It's a valid question. Signs of his future courage show up throughout Ray's upbringing in India, including one story he tells about an incident with a large group of violent people which taught him to think on his feet in order to survive.

Ray's family is from a higher caste in India, castes being a hierarchical system which organizes Indian society based on birth and birth alone. While this system is not officially recognized in modern times, and is even illegal in places, it still promotes inequality for those born at the bottom of the castes, who are known as "untouchables." Ray's caste, on the other hand, consists of "rich people, business people," he says. "Doctors and educated people."

When he was about twenty-four years of age, Ray tells a story which began as a peaceful night with a couple of his friends. As they relaxed, drinking tea in the streets of their neighborhood, one of Ray's friends revealed he had loaned money to someone who hadn't paid it back. Whether it was pride or the young Ray Khan's testosterone kicking in, the small group of friends entered the untouchable's compound in an attempt to retrieve their friend's cash. When they found the debtor and asked for the money to be returned, things went decidedly sideways.

"He suddenly screaming that they beat him, they kill him," Ray recounts. "Hundreds of people around us with knives and scissors. Men, women—suddenly the people were beating us."

As Ray recalls the events of that night, he says he and his friends were sure they were going to get killed. In an early move which foreshadowed the bravery at his very core, Ray says he realized one of his friends had brought a gun with him. Ray says he grabbed the gun and pointed it at the ground, telling people to leave and brandishing it as the group made their escape. When one guy started yelling "you want to kill me, kill me," Ray says he fired the gun at the dirt next to the man, eventually creating enough space for him and his friends to get out.

When asked if he was scared during this incident, Ray simply shrugs. "Maybe they would have killed us," he says. "But they just don't understand."

"I've seen him in situations like that and he's not afraid," Valoze says as he listens to Ray's story.

An incident such as this might provoke a range of emotions in those of us from the West, but things are different in India, as Ray will tell you. And Ray brought this relaxed attitude with him each day he worked with the ATF.

"Sometimes we get like good, good people, like bad, bad people, like very bad history," Ray says. With a nod to his story mentioned above, Ray adds, "No, never ever scared of them. They always scared of me."

CHAPTER FOUR

During Operation Ceasefire, there were numerous undercover agents from across the country who came to South Georgia to assist with the operation. They would usually stay for a few weeks and assist with the day-to-day operations, jumping right in to purchase contraband from bad guys. One of these agents was Darius Lewis out of the ATF Detroit office. Darius was a great undercover agent who was always the first to show up and the last to leave. When Darius got to town, he jumped in with the undercover crew at the undercover operation, seamlessly fitting in and conversing with the targets right off the bat. He was introduced to the targets as the crew's main Detroit connection, a hustler who assisted in transporting and selling firearms to Canadian clients. On his second day at the operation, he began purchasing narcotics and firearms from the individuals coming into the store. Agent Valoze let him do his thing, knowing he was an experienced undercover who knew the job well and wrote good investigative reports which detailed his activities.

By the end of his first week, Darius had started dealing with two young gangbangers who were selling powder cocaine. He purchased a small amount from them, and they were talking a big game to him, as gangbangers often do, telling him they dealt in large weight. These two youngsters were members of a larger gang Ray Khan had brought to the operation. With Valoze busy on other purchases, Ray introduced the two men to Darius.

Through the course of their transactions, the two men told Darius they could deliver a half-kilo of cocaine for $7,000 the next week. Darius told them he would get back to them, and he explained the situation to Agent Valoze, asking him if the money was available. Valoze explained to him that they weren't really trying to spend big chunks of their evidence purchase money on drugs, as they were trying to save it for guns. Valoze also expressed concern about these two young targets, telling Darius several of these young gangsters had tried to sell them low purity and fake cocaine in the past. Darius responded that the cocaine he had already purchased from these youngsters was high quality and he felt good about this deal. Valoze could tell that he really wanted to do this deal before he returned to Detroit, and because Darius had always come through for him, he told him he would find the funds for the half-kilo.

The next week, Valoze obtained the funds and told Darius to go ahead and order the cocaine. Darius reached out to the targets and arranged to purchase the dope on Friday morning. He was headed back to Detroit that evening. The young gangsters actually showed up on time with a neatly packaged half-kilo. Valoze and the rest of the undercover crew were conducting a short-barreled shotgun purchase at the same time that Darius's deal was happening, so they couldn't participate. The gangsters provided Darius with a small sample (a few grams) to accompany the half-kilo. Darius said everything looked good and he exchanged $7,000 in official buy money for the half-kilo.

That Friday turned out to be a busy day with numerous transactions, and all the evidence was placed into the temporary safe until the end of the day. Valoze drove Darius to the airport and dropped him off, thanking him for his help. On the way back, Valoze received a call from one of the Glynn County detectives who was working in the cover room. The detective told Agent Valoze that she had opened the half-kilo to conduct a field test and that it didn't look or smell right to her. And she was an experienced narcotics investigator. She informed Valoze the half-kilo appeared to be primarily consisted of "cut," probably lidocaine. The sample she removed from the package had barely tested positive. All the narcotics the team purchased were sent to the Drug Enforcement Administration (DEA) lab for official testing, to include purity testing. The detective told Valoze she suspected this substance to be less than 10 percent pure. Valoze sighed, telling her that he would handle the situation.

This had happened before on a few occasions. If you buy enough dope off the streets, eventually someone is going to try to rip you off, either with drugs that primarily consist of cut or are just straight up bunk (fake drugs). For an undercover agent, it's a matter of personal pride when this happens. Nobody likes to be ripped off. And if you don't do anything about it, your street credibility is out the door.

Over the weekend, Valoze called Darius and filled him in on the situation. Darius was extremely apologetic and angry at the same time. Valoze understood. It was hard not to take these things personally. He told Darius not to sweat it, that it happens to everyone eventually. Valoze only requested that he call the two youngsters and raise hell, telling them that they needed to make this right. Valoze told him to tell them he hadn't opened the package until he returned to Detroit, and that when he did, he realized that they had sold him some bullshit. Darius also planned to tell them that he wanted to resell the half-kilo for a profit and if he had tried to sell that shit, it could have gotten him killed.

Valoze knew too well that when this happened, the odds of getting the buy money back were close to zero. The best he could hope for was that the drug dealers would at least attempt to make things right by providing some legitimate cocaine. Valoze decided that, instead of trying to find these two punks and confronting them directly, it would be better to go directly to the leader of this gang and present his case. After all, Ray Khan brought them to the store, and they had been making money from the agents by selling guns and drugs. They wouldn't want that gravy train to stop. So Valoze reached out to Ray and briefed him on the situation. He asked Ray to reach out to the gang leader, to tell him what had happened, and to request a meeting with Valoze. Ray simply responded:

"Sir, I will make this right. It will be handled properly, sir."

And Valoze knew that with Ray on the job, it would be.

That Monday, Ray arrived at the store early in the afternoon and told Valoze the gang leader would be there in a few minutes. The name of this gang was the Piru, and the leader went by the name of "X." The agents learned his actual name was Xavier. Valoze had personally conducted two undercover transactions with X after Ray made the introduction. Both transactions involved stolen firearms. Most of the members of the Piru gang that X brought with him into the warehouse were young, between the ages of sixteen and twenty. The agents didn't like dealing with these young gang members as they seemed to always cause the most problems in these undercover operations. They were prone to violence, would frequently try to rob or burglarize the business after hours, and had no problem trying to rip off the undercovers. That's just the way that they handled themselves.

Shortly after he spoke to Ray, X arrived at the warehouse. He had two of his crew with him, but it was not the two who had ripped off Darius. Ray suggested to X that he come outside and speak with him and Valoze in his vehicle, and X agreed. Valoze hadn't expected Ray to do that, but he was good with it because he didn't necessarily want this conversation to be recorded. So, X, Ray, and Valoze went outside and sat in Ray's Escalade.

Ray took the lead, explaining to X that his two crew members' actions were going to jeopardize the relationship between his gang and himself and Sal. Ray further stated that no member of the gang would be welcome in the business if things weren't made right. Ray was all business, sounding more and more like a gangster himself. Valoze hadn't said a word yet. X stated he had not sanctioned this sale by these two members and had not even been made aware of the transaction. He went on to state that he appreciated this relationship and did not want it to end. He asked Valoze what he needed to do to make things right.

Ray jumped in, answering for Valoze, "You need to bring the agreed-upon amount of cocaine to us by tomorrow."

At this point, Valoze told X that he was a businessman, and he and his team were all about maintaining a good business relationship with their clients. What X's two young associates had done was really bad for the relationship between X's people and Sal's business, and it needed to be made right. Valoze told X that he respected him and that, because of their relationship, he wanted to resolve this issue peacefully. He told him this was why he had requested the meeting with X: out of respect.

Then Ray chimed in. "It must be resolved quickly."

X shook Valoze's hand and assured him that he was going to handle this matter within a few days. He got out of the Escalade and motioned to his two associates that it was time to go.

Two days went by, and nothing was seen or heard from the Piru gang at the undercover operation. Usually, a day didn't go by without at least a few of them coming into the store. Ray seemed to be taking this personally, as well, and he assured Valoze that he would have things taken care of by the end of the week. Valoze, however, had pretty much given up hope and had moved on. This shit happened. It wasn't the end of the world.

The next day, Ray showed up to the warehouse with X and a few Piru members. To the agents' dismay, they all arrived together in Ray's Escalade. One of X's gang members approached Valoze at the counter and handed him a large package of powder cocaine. Valoze knew it wasn't even close to a half kilo, but it was a sizable amount. Valoze weighed the drugs on a digital scale, and it weighed out to just under a quarter-kilo. This was definitely more than Valoze expected. He looked over at Ray, who appeared to be extremely proud of himself.

X looked at Valoze. "We good?"

Valoze paused, having mixed emotions. Deep down, he had already chalked up the whole situation as a loss. But due to Ray Khan's efforts, X attempted to right this wrong. Although what he had provided was only half of what had been agreed upon, and legally it probably couldn't be attributed to the original Piru members who ripped off Darius, it was still an effort. In truth, it was much more than Valoze had expected. X also quickly added that he had banned the two youngsters from coming into the store and doing any further business.

Valoze shook X's hand. "We good."

X and his crew left the store. Ray couldn't wipe the smile off his face as he walked out behind them, just beaming with pride. Valoze yelled out to Ray that he needed him to return to the store immediately after he dropped them off. About thirty minutes later, Ray returned to the store, expecting a hero's welcome. Valoze pulled him aside. "You did a good job, but you have to be smarter than that."

"What do you mean, sir?' Ray asked, completely taken aback. He thought he'd killed it by bringing the gang members back and getting them to basically give the agents a bunch of cocaine.

"You absolutely cannot drive your vehicle around with a bunch of gangsters and a large amount of cocaine in it," Valoze told his informant. "They are all convicted felons, and I'm sure they all have guns on them. That is enough dope to put you all in prison for ten years. What if you had gotten pulled over by the police?" Valoze asked.

"Sir, that would never happen. I am very careful, sir," Ray assured him.

"Careful? You didn't call me, so I had no idea you were going to do that. If you had gotten pulled over, that might have been the end of this operation, and there was probably nothing I could do to help you. You do realize that I am barely able to keep you in this country right now, don't you? One more arrest and your ass will be back in India." Valoze hated being so direct with the man who brought them so many criminals, but it was clear to Ray that he was genuinely concerned for his safety.

Ray, typically, was unfazed. "Sir, you have great power, and we could have explained all of that. We made things right and now they will sell us more guns!"

Valoze could only smile and shake his head. Ray just didn't understand the way the American legal system worked. But his confidence was off the charts, and Valoze respected that.

"You did a great job, Ray. Just don't be giving any more rides to any of our future defendants. I can't afford to lose you," Valoze said, his voice finally softening.

"Sir, yes, sir."

Despite his apparent cockiness, from this point Ray never let people sit in his car. Instead, they would follow him to the warehouse. Given Agent Valoze's warning, he was now scared to get pulled over with dope in the car.

"And they follow me and that time I tell them [the agents], this car number [license plate] is this and they come behind me. And I text it to them all the time and they have a bag of some kind of medicine they call ecstasy. And Lou Sir did the deal."

As Valoze will tell you, he didn't get into the weeds regarding Ray's techniques when he was away from the warehouse. Some things you just don't want to know.

"ATF loved the results so much they didn't care about the methods," he says. "Those were the type of guys that he [Ray] was getting us into. We never would have been able to get into them otherwise."

Ray nods, and then adds, "I go with them sometimes, bad guys, I go with them strip club, too, because they say, 'come on to strip club to talk.'"

"Ray, you love strip clubs," Valoze teases.

Even Ray's mahogany cheek blushes a little as he grins. "Oh no, no. I have to, no I don't go to strip clubs," he protests as the two share a laugh. Their history is clear whenever they are together: a shared past bonding the two men more strongly than the expected agent-informant relationship. As they reminisce about other strip clubs they have visited (apparently there was a great one in Miami), it becomes clear Valoze is grateful for Ray's presence in his life, not just his career, and is well aware of the sacrifices his informant has made.

While Ray was in Brunswick three days each week, drumming up business for the ATF's operation, his convenience stores were finally thriving. By that time, he had a full-time employee running his Statesboro store and another working his lease in Vidalia. He was starting to build his businesses up but, being Ray, he still went to each store every weekday to make sure things were running as planned. And they were. This didn't stop Ray from trying to make another quick buck here and there, though. And sometimes, this small greed got him into trouble.

Along with the three-lane shooting range, the shelves and counters of Valoze's warehouse had to be filled in order to make the surplus business appear real. Agent Valoze and his team were able to appropriate palettes full of bootlegged DVDs (some of them were regular movies and some were pornographic), surplus military equipment, and counterfeit clothing and purses. There were, of course, untaxed cigarettes as well. Most of this stock came through Tom Lesnak and, except for the cigarettes, all these items were worthless. Being counterfeit, the items legally had no value at all.

"There was lots of porn, for some reason," Valoze remembers. "One time Sonny [one of Valoze's undercover partners during Ceasefire] traded a box of bootlegged porn for a gun." As far as the agents were concerned, they'd gotten this particular firearm off the streets for free.

During their interactions with the lowlifes and potential defendants who visited the warehouse, the agents mostly gave the disks away. Otherwise, Ray took them from the warehouse to use them as bait. He had free access to the shelves, and, as he was doing so well for them, the ATF agents didn't care what Ray took from their storage. Daily, he went into the neighborhoods around Brunswick, handing out bootlegged movies, porn, and other counterfeit material goods.

As Ray says, "Everyone is talking to me normal and talking about the guns and drugs. I went every day to all the neighborhoods, every day. Brunswick is too small, so all kinds of people know me. 'Ray! Ray!' They offer me tea and coffee, too. I just say my manager is from New York and in order to get more cigarettes from the New York in at cheaper price, I ask them to sell to the Lou Sir guns for New York. And we transport guns to New York and get more cigarettes and more of this good stuff."

Ever on the lookout for ways to make a quick buck, however, Ray brought some of the merchandise from the warehouse and put it in his stores. Ray says he put the DVDs there to draw in people who would be interested in them, and he would tell his employees to then redirect them to his "big store" in Brunswick where they could talk to Ray about more product. Ray will tell you he never meant for those DVDs to be sold.

"Only the bad people looked at those shelves," according to Ray. "Good people never did."

Had Ray told the ATF agents he was putting these DVDs in his stores, they would have told him not to. They would also say it wasn't a big deal because, at the same time, Ray was bringing in guys with machine guns. It really wasn't a big deal… unless you were the Department of Revenue, and specifically, Billy Thompson.

The DOR were regularly included in ATF's undercover location–based investigations. They even sent some of their agents to work at the sites on occasion. DOR needed to be on board to help with licensing and some of the financial considerations for the cases. In Brunswick, for example, Thunderbolt Surplus was selling cigarettes and had a tobacco license in Ray Khan's and Sal Nunziato's names. Thompson approved the license himself and knew the whole time that this business was an undercover operation. He knew what Ray was doing for the operation, and he knew the ways in which he was helping in this federal investigation.

Perhaps Ray's successful involvement pricked Thompson, considering his lost charges in Statesboro, or perhaps it was the continued influence of Nital Patel. Whatever the reason, while Ceasefire was in motion, Thompson was spearheading further investigations into Ray's stores.

When you ask him about Ray's next arrest, this time for selling bootlegged DVDs in his store, Agent Valoze will once again revert to one of his favorite phrases: "It was chicken shit." He'll go on to say people were overdosing and shooting each other in Georgia, but the Department of Revenue spent their time investigating the sale of pirated DVDs. Agent Valoze will also tell you Thompson was part of a pervasive and powerful Good Ol' Boys network, which he says operated throughout the state of Georgia. Thompson himself was a Bulloch County boy and was still pissed off about the US Attorney's involvement in dropping Ray's gambling charges, so he used his influence to keep investigators focused on Ray's businesses.

"Department of Revenue, Thompson, they were very involved in our operation because they gave us the wholesale tobacco license," Valoze says. "They had full knowledge of everything that was happening. A Department of Revenue guy was there a couple days a week, working in the cover room with us. So, they were very involved in this operation. They knew everything Ray was doing. But the whole time, unbeknownst to us, they're fucking investigating him. Ray was Thompson's Moby Dick and Thompson was fucking Ahab [...] So, it's just a weird situation when you think about it."

In December of 2009, an undercover Bulloch County deputy went into Ray's Statesboro store and purchased some of the pirated DVD movies. Between October of 2009 and February 2010, undercover officers also bought bootleg DVDs from the store in Vidalia. In January 2010, the same month that Agent Valoze purchased his fiftieth firearm at Thunderbolt Surplus (a feat which would never have occurred without Ray's involvement), an arrest warrant was once again issued for Ray. He was arrested in Toombs County in April on state racketeering (RICO) and gambling charges. During a search warrant at his Statesboro store, over six hundred pirated DVDs were located. A second felony warrant was later issued for Ray in Bulloch County related to the DVDs in his Vidalia location, triggering the revocation of Ray's pre-trial diversion and reinstatement of the previously deferred prosecution.

"They come to my Statesboro store and took it, all my stuff, and put it in the news, and I was in the jail inside," Ray says of this incident. "I don't know why are they doing all this stuff."

Ray Khan remained in custody in Toombs County, ineligible for bond due to the Bulloch County arrest warrant, as he awaited his court dates. It was at this point that he met William Larson, a district attorney overseeing prosecutions in Toombs County, and another Georgia Good Ol' Boy.

"This is how things work in South Georgia," Valoze says, referring to visits Larson made to Ray while he was incarcerated.

"It all happened in small rooms in the courthouse," Ray recalls, "not in front of a judge. That William Larson, that guy asked me for three hundred thousand dollars."

Ray is referring to several visits he received from Larson during the many weeks he spent at the Toombs County Jail. "He would ask me to pay three hundred thousand dollars in fines," Ray says. "Every ten days or so, he was coming back and ask me again. He would just send me back to jail."

When you ask Ray if the Department of Revenue were looking into him, he'll initially deny it. For some reason, Ray tried to mitigate the targeted investigation Valoze sees looking back on that time. Instead, Ray will say, "They were not looking, but they try to give me a hard time. Because of this William Larson. Because they wants to support my brother-in-law, so they wants to put me inside jail to get my money."

Indeed, while Ray was in jail, he received a surprise visit from his brother-in-law, Nital Patel, who, you will understand by this point in our story, was more than aware of Ray's current legal troubles. While Ray was incarcerated, his businesses were suffering. Ray had little trust in his employees at the best of times, and they certainly didn't know how to keep the stores afloat in his absence. They had no access to his business accounts or the skills to manage the accounting and inventories. Needless to say, Ray was vulnerable—and Nital used this opportunity to his advantage.

"My brother-in-law, when I was in jail, he came to me and he say, 'Give me power of attorney and all.' I just sign it, and then he took my bank money and everything. I don't have nothing. No money. Even he changed my title to my Cadillac to his name," Ray says. "And when I came back, I told him, 'Give me at least my Cadillac so I can do something.' I thought I have some money in my savings account and all, but he took it. And I say, 'Where is my gas station?' And he say, 'Gas station totally run down, and I spend lot of money and it's not making money, so you have to give me money.' I say, 'I don't have anything, man.' He took everything. He just said, like, he lost so much money to run my gas station, so I have to give him money. He asking me for money."

Ray's incredulity is clear. Stuck inside the Toombs County Jail, and despite his hesitation, Ray tried to put his trust in someone else. In a family member. His own sister's husband. But, whether through ineptitude or malice, Nital ran Ray's businesses into the ground. He emptied Ray's accounts. And, to top it all off, Ray lost another Cadillac, which he would have to watch being driven by someone else. Again.

Because of his incarceration, Agent Valoze lost Ray's assistance for the last few months of Operation Ceasefire—his most successful undercover operation to date. At this point, however, Valoze says Ray had brought in so many quality defendants and set up so many undercover purchases that their operation was rolling on its own at that point.

"We were knee-deep in guns and narcotics and suspects," he says. "Ray had absolutely crushed it."

You can see his regret when he thinks back on his actions—or lack thereof—at this time, but Agent Valoze will admit he didn't do much to help Ray at this point. There really wasn't much he could have done. Ray was now locked up on multiple state charges with a federal ICE detainer on him, and Valoze was overwhelmed with the paperwork and operational planning leading to the end of Operation Ceasefire. But still, Valoze knows now that Ray deserved better from him. He deserved more.

"It wasn't my shining moment," he says, "but Ceasefire was ending and the takedown was set for early summer."

Unfortunately, this isn't an uncommon outcome for many federal informants. As former ATF agent Tom Lesnak will tell you, regardless of the operation, "in the end, there wasn't a single source which didn't get absolutely fucked." He goes on to say, "[I have] other informants who have emigrated from India, lived in their gas station for three years. They come over to work their asses off and then bring their families."

One of Lesnak's informants was even put on the terror watch list. "He's pulling in truckloads of fentanyl, kilos of cocaine, and he does it by flying around the world for his legitimate business," Lesnak says. "And they grounded him in a case of mistaken identity. You think the government helped him?" is Lesnak's rhetorical question.

"At the end of the day, we [the government] didn't honor our commitment to Ray and to other people who did this," Lesnak says, shaking his head at the injustice. "At the end of the day, these guys all get fucked. At the end of the day, we don't hold up our promises. And it's not at our level."

During the massive round-up for Ceasefire, tactical units kicked in the doors of over ninety defendants from the operation. There were several shoot-outs during the raids, and one of the defendants' cousins, who thought it was a drug bust, exchanged fire with the SWAT unit and was killed. Clearly, Ray and the ATF agents had been dealing with some very violent people, and the tactical teams were not taking any chances. Flash-bangs, armored vehicles, and no-knock warrants were utilized for some of the apprehensions. It was a massive takedown and word spread quickly through the area. The criminal underbelly soon learned that Thunderbolt Surplus was a sting operation, and its employees were all undercover federal agents and informants. It was a dangerous time for everyone involved.

Agent Valoze was not present for the Ceasefire takedown. He always hated those parts of the operations. Valoze felt like he had created genuine connections with some of the people who would be going to prison as a result of knowing him, and sometimes he knew their spouses and children as well. Unfortunately, this was the price of a deep undercover operation. He also knew another operation was looming, but he was burned out and his family needed to see him, even for just a short time.

Operation Ceasefire and its agents (read "the brass"—special agents in charge, the US Attorney's Office, and the like) would be recognized as the 2009 Organized Crime Drug Enforcement Task Forces (OCDETF) case of the year. As a result of Operation Ceasefire, ninety-one arrests were made. Of these, fifty-seven defendants were charged with federal firearms and narcotics violations. Valoze had more important matters on his mind than the man who had brought in more than eighty of these defendants. To his credit, he recognizes his faults in hindsight. He'll tell you he should have done better by Ray.

"Why was nothing done to help the poor CI sitting in Toombs County Jail?" you might ask. A valid question.

Valoze has an answer for you: "The sheriffs are like emperors down there, with total power. Only way they lose their power is through FBI arrest for corruption."

At this time, Ray and Agent Valoze estimate there were "thirty or forty" gas stations and their owners facing "civil charges" in southern Georgia. All these charges were relating to civil forfeitures, like the one Ray was facing with Larson's $300,000 fine. Sadly, this practice would not come to light until several years later.

For example, in a March 29, 2018, news article about Thomas Oglethorpe, Larson's brother-in-law who was assigned to act as a member of President Trump's legal defense team, news agency WRAL reveals Oglethorpe and Larson "were contracted to work for several district attorneys and targeted owners and operators of businesses accused of allowing illegal gambling on coin-operated machines. The two seized assets while prosecuting the cases and paid themselves so-called 'contingency fees' from those assets." The article goes on to say that "in May 2012, state Attorney General Sam Olens issued an executive order cracking down on contingency fees." And later, "In July 2012, the state Court of Appeals agreed that such contingency fees violate public policy, creating a conflict of interest for district attorneys who have a financial stake in a defendant's conviction."

From this it seems apparent that Ray was caught up in a much larger scheme of corruption and profit run by the rich and powerful in South Georgia—a network Valoze says was still going strong when he retired from ATF in 2017. As he sat in jail in 2010, however, and was repeatedly denied bond due to his charges in Bulloch County, Ray endured repeated visits from Larson and continued demands for a $300,000 fine.

"And I say I don't have money and all this—that much money," Ray recalls. "And I don't want to lie to you [he told Larson]. I can give you some money after twenty days or fifty days. And he say, 'How about two months? Sixty days? You can get it?' I say, 'Yes,' and then he going to let me go."

In total, Ray sat in the Toombs County Jail for seventy-seven days until he finally pled guilty to the state charges of Commercial Gambling (a felony), Keeping a Gambling Place, and Possession of Gambling Device or Equipment (both misdemeanors) on July 22, 2010. He also agreed to pay Larson's loosely defined "fine." However, Ray was not yet free. No indeed. Although his state charges had been dealt with, ICE now needed their pound of flesh.

On August 9, 2010, Ray was transferred into federal custody and sent to the Enforcement Removal Operations (ERO) facility in anticipation of his removal from the United States. When considering this next governmental betrayal of Ray Khan, we should note some important facts about ICE, who placed this new detainer on Ray: (1) ICE was part of Operation Ceasefire; (2) an ICE agent came to the business every week; (3) ICE agents worked with all of the other agents and officers on the operation and saw the types of people Ray brought into the store; (4) ICE knew that Ray was at the Ceasefire store every day and knew he spent little time working at these gas stations, so had little control over what merchandise his employees sold.

And yet, despite all of ICE's knowledge of Ray's value, loyalty, and contributions to a huge federal case, this federal agency failed to balance what Ray was doing against the purpose of the detainer. The entire ICE chain of command ultimately failed to stand up for Ray Khan.

All of Ray's dreams were scheduled to crumble on November 5, 2010—the date for his deportation back to India.

CHAPTER FIVE

The official start date for the next ATF undercover case, Operation Crossbones, was August 9, 2010. Agent Valoze will tell you, however, that nothing really happened in this investigation until he could once again get Ray Khan out of custody and back working as his informant. Until that happened, Valoze and his team were stuck using another ATF informant, a white guy who was immersed in the criminal world and claimed he had contacts in the underground network of cigarette trafficking. Unfortunately, for the early days of Operation Crossbones, these claims proved to be false.

Valoze and his team really didn't have any interest in the trafficking of untaxed cigarettes, but it had become a means to an end in these types of operations. It was a great backstop, showing criminals who came to the warehouse that the undercover agents were involved in a complex scheme of criminal activity. It was also an efficient way to fund the operations through what is known as law enforcement "churning" authority. This allowed the agents to utilize money made by selling the untaxed cigarettes to pay some of the expenses involved in running these high-price operations. As a benefit, agents could also level federal charges on those engaged in this illegal activity. There was huge potential for profit in selling untaxed cigarettes to Ray's associates. But at this point, Ray was stuck in an ICE holding facility and calling Agent Valoze every chance he had.

"Lou Sir, but you have great power," Ray would tell him during every call. As a lowly street-level ATF agent, however, there just wasn't much Valoze could do.

While Ray dealt with his federal immigration charges, it was becoming clear that, without him, this new operation would not start well. Because of issues with other ATF warehouse operations around the country, Valoze decided this new operation would not be open to the general public. The success of the operation was now entirely dependent on the informant's ability to bring high-level criminals to the warehouse. This new informant, although he talked a big game, had only produced a few low-level stragglers who were selling small amounts of narcotics. This was not how Valoze had envisioned his new project would start.

Despite his own burnout, Agent Valoze had quickly been drawn back into this next operation. Based on his successes with the three prior undercover operations in Georgia, he ensured his bosses this would be one of the most successful undercover warehouse operations ever conducted. No pressure. Valoze was also aiming higher with this new investigation. Instead of street-level dope dealers, he wanted to focus mainly on crime guns—and lots of them. In selling the new operation to the ATF, he crafted a vision of taking down transnational organizations involved in high-level money laundering, narcotics distribution, and the trafficking of firearms.

Valoze knew that, with Ray at his side, he could deliver. However, when Valoze had been making such bold predictions to his supervisors, Ray Khan had been a free man, and the agent was relying on his full participation. As each of the previous investigations ended, ATF's higher-ups had basked in the publicity created through the operations' numbers, so they were totally on board.

The business and locations involved in Operation Ceasefire were completely burned. Everyone in the community (particularly in the criminal underbelly) knew it had been a front for a federal sting. The agents needed a fresh start in a new city, so they relocated to the small town of Thunderbolt, Georgia, which is adjacent to Savannah. Valoze had already obtained a commercial warehouse in Thunderbolt to store the overflow of swag and cigarettes during Operation Ceasefire. The warehouse had a front office and was in an industrial area. It was clean, so Valoze decided to use it as the primary location for Operation Crossbones.

Once again, ATF would require the backing and support of the Georgia Department of Revenue to maintain their undercover tobacco retail license. Once this licensure was secured, the DOR also approved the bulk purchase of cigarettes. Having this merchandise in their warehouse gave credibility to the undercover identities of the agents—and the wholesale business itself. Again, these cigarettes would arrive untaxed, which had proved fruitful in previous operations.

As with Operation Ceasefire, ATF agents were again joined by Department of Revenue agents, who assisted in monitoring the cover room on at least a weekly basis. These DOR agents and their supervisors had full knowledge of the entire ATF operation. Later, however, when questioned by the Office of the Inspector

General (OIG), these agents and Billy Thompson himself would deny any knowledge of the sale of untaxed cigarettes—but more on this later. ATF would also be supported by the Savannah-Chatham Metropolitan Police Department (SCMPD), one of their officers would be embedded into the business in an undercover capacity alongside the ATF agents.

Things did not go well for the first month of the operation. Agent Valoze and his team felt increasing pressure from their chains of command to perform, and it just wasn't happening. The new CI wasn't using the untaxed cigarettes effectively to bring in the people he promised. It was becoming clear he did not have the contacts in this world he claimed when offered the opportunity to work off his charges. This isn't uncommon when using informants in an investigation, but it became detrimental for Valoze in the early weeks of Crossbones. Unlike their previous locations, the warehouse was not open to the public, which eliminated the foot traffic they benefited from in the previous operations.

"I get this informant, a white guy," Valoze recalls, "who kind of dabbles in the cigarette business a little bit. And now we're putting ourselves out there as a wholesale tobacco warehouse at the start of this operation and we have nothing going on. We're getting no fucking business. And, you know, my whole team is telling me, 'You gotta get fuckin' Ray. We gotta get Ray Khan out.'"

Agent Valoze admits, if this new informant had been productive, he probably wouldn't have jumped through all the hoops necessary to get Ray released from ICE custody. But it was becoming clear that Operation Crossbones needed Ray Khan.

The next time he called, Valoze could be honest with Ray—he really was doing everything he could to get him released. As a former Homeland Security Investigations (HSI) agent himself, Valoze was now pulling every number he had out of a dusty address book and calling all the ICE contacts he knew.

Ray's response was typical: "Sir, you can do it. You have great power." This was how Ray was. To Agent Valoze, when looking back on these times, it seemed Ray somehow willed things to happen. And they did.

As November 5, 2010, loomed, and Ray's deportation came ever closer, Agent Valoze, his boss, and the US Attorney's Office began filling out the interminable paperwork to try to keep Ray in the country. Like the countdown in a thriller movie, Ray's time in the United States ticked away, day by day, hour by hour, and he was powerless to do anything about it. On November 1, an official ATF request for Ray to remain was finally submitted. Ironically, the request was supported by the same ICE agent who put the detainer on him in the first place—the same agent who worked with Ray and Valoze during Ceasefire. It was, quite literally, the very least he could do. Regardless of this request, Valoze says it ultimately took Valoze's call to a high-ranking previous HSI colleague to "help with the red tape and get him out."

Just in the nick of time, on November 3, 2010, ICE halted Ray's deportation. This decision was made following an ATF request which recognized Ray's previous criminal history but also acknowledged the low severity of his purported crimes. The documentation specified that Ray would be useful in a federal investigation involving a significant number of foreign nationals. Little did anyone know at the time that this would turn out to be a massive understatement.

Even without this knowledge of the future, however, HSI took notice of ATF's application and suspended Ray's imminent departure. Ray's charges in Bulloch County had fortunately been dropped pending his imminent deportation, and on December 6, 2010, ATF took custody of Ray Khan for twelve months so he could assist with Operation Crossbones. In the ways of the federal government, however, Ray remained at the ICE facility while the details of this exchange were ironed out. As he awaited his release, Ray continued to call Agent Valoze. Despite only being permitted one call a day, he used it, without fail, to call Valoze. Every. Fucking. Day. Valoze says he always took Ray's call, despite having nothing to tell him. Ray's mantra remained true: "You have great power."

On January 6, 2011, Agent Valoze spoke to Ray, who was still incarcerated at the ICE facility. Despite assuring him of his imminent release, Valoze says Ray was (understandably) anxious and at his wits' end. Valoze says this was probably the only time he can remember Ray showing any measure of concern. Finally, on January 20, 2011, Agent Valoze received word from HSI that Ray's release would occur within a week. This came as a huge relief to Ray, who was done being held in jail, but also to Valoze, whose operation was floundering without Ray's contributions.

Agent Valoze put every resource he had into this new case. Money, agents, locations, merchandise, and the expectations of his chain of command all depended on his success. There was no way, however, that Valoze could hope to cultivate a new informant on Ray's level. They simply did not exist. Yet it still wasn't until February 2, 2011, when Ray was finally freed. He was placed in ATF custody, specifically, in the charge of Agents Valoze and Ralf Bicknese, Valoze's partner in Operation Crossbones.

The ICE facility was in Atlanta, four hours away from Valoze's current location. For that reason, Agent Valoze contacted a friend, ATF agent Daniel "Gooch" Arrugueta, and asked him to pick Ray up and take him to a hotel in Atlanta. He needed to be released into ATF's custody, and it may come as no surprise, but ICE was not willing to transport Ray anywhere. That night, Gooch called his friend.

"You fucking owe me, man," Gooch said to Valoze. "That motherfucker smelled so bad I need to go get my G-ride detailed."

There was simply no way for Agent Arrugueta to remove the stench Ray, having spent several months in an ICE facility, left in his car. Valoze truly did owe his friend. Big time.

When you ask Ray about his release, after spending all those months in custody, he recalls telling Gooch, "Drop me off where they have very nice bar. Take me to Marriott." And who can blame him?

Once he was freed, Ray faced a new reality: He once again had nothing. Nital had bankrupted his stores, drained his savings accounts, and even took his car. In true Ray Khan fashion, however, he faced this new challenge head on.

"I just move out from there [Brunswick] to the Savannah," Ray tells me. "And I told the Lou Sir, 'If I work here every day, then how can I survive?' I have to do something, or I can work somewhere, like the employee at the gas station for ten dollars, twelve dollars, but I cannot come here every day. So Lou Sir say, 'Let me figure it out,' and then we talk to the Tom Sir [then–ATF agent Tom Lesnak] and he say, 'How about we can give you some cigarettes at the cheaper price with the like tax stamp on them and everything, then you can sell it and you can make the money off it and you can rent your house and everything?' And I have work then. Tom Sir gifted me one white minivan."

Agent Lesnak set Ray up with this van in which he could load legal tobacco products. These were provided through Lesnak's own warehouse operation, which functioned on a worldwide scale. Valoze recalls that his colleague's operation supported numerous undercover missions throughout the United States at this time. Through Lesnak's suppliers, Ray's legal tobacco supply would be supplemented by the usual untaxed products, which he could use as bait when he was out doing what Ray Khan does.

"After a couple of deals," Lesnak says, "the bad guys want more, so you have to be willing to do legitimate transactions first. That led to illegitimate transactions. This helped to avoid entrapment."

Lesnak's undercover operation was seven years long, which was completely unheard of. "That's because we had people like Ray who literally did the shit, dirty work," he says. "They never told anyone what was going on."

Lesnak goes on to emphasize the importance of incorporating real businessmen, like Ray, into undercover investigations of this type. "Ninety percent of our business was one hundred percent legitimate," Lesnak says. "You needed a legitimate businessman as a front, to teach you. We seized businesses because these smart businessmen knew how the businesses worked. Legitimate businessmen lead you into the criminal organizations. Too many of our guys don't know how to handle informants, and most don't know how to handle those who are smarter than us."

In his long-term operations, Lesnak says he would bring informants in for their skill level and their access. He says there was no way agents would be able to infiltrate the types of criminal enterprises their investigations targeted as they simply don't have access to them. Unfortunately, this also means the handlers of these confidential informants must sometimes defer to them, whilst also trying to keep them in their lane. "You know it's going to be different depending on the informant," Lesnak says. "Most of my cooperators were not defendants. It's different when dealing with them. You have less leverage."

This was not the case for Agent Valoze, who completely trusted Ray Khan to infiltrate the local community he knew best. While this level of confidence in an informant might be unusual, Lesnak shares Valoze's memories of the ways Ray worked, having used Ray in several of his cases, as well. "I regularly pulled Ray around the country to help in various operations," he recalls.

From the agents' collective memories, it is clear that, although Ray had his immigration-based motivations for working, he was truly one of a kind. And once again, when he was dropped into Crossbones, he excelled.

"So, we would sell…how many fucking cases?" Valoze asks Ray.

"Thousands. Every day come flatbed truck."

"We'd do a hundred-thousand-dollar deal and that goes into the kitty," Valoze says. "And because we were putting ourselves out there as big time now, we'd buy brand new cars and trucks that we drove. We had to act as though we were now operating as very high-level criminals."

Agent Valoze and Ray Khan would work together on Operation Crossbones for the next three years. Every month, Valoze was required to file further paperwork to his chain of command, justifying Ray's custodial situation and his continued productivity in the investigation, but this was no hard task. Ray, as usual, hit the ground running.

"We get him out and Ray immediately comes and starts working for us," Valoze says. "And now, that's when he took us to another level. Like a whole other fucking level. Now I am putting myself out there as a freight forwarder. We really kicked it up a notch on this one. Now I'm not driving a hoopty anymore, I'm driving a brand-new Jaguar."

Valoze remembers that other case agents and management didn't necessarily approve of these new cars. "We needed the street cred at that higher level," Valoze says. "We needed the bad guys to think we were legitimately in the game, on a big scale, and there's no way we were affiliated with law enforcement."

Ray nods along as Valoze recalls the early days of Crossbones. "Everyone got the new car," he adds. "We sold like thousands of dollars of cigarettes every day. Because that's what I know how to do, sell stuff."

By this time, Ray remarried and his new wife and his son from his previous marriage came to Savannah with him. "Now I live in Savannah at that time, 'cause…I used to live in Statesboro, but I just come to there because it's too far to go every day, so I come to the Savannah and rent a house there."

While he was grateful to be close to his family again, when it came to bringing in people for the ATF operation, Ray needed to start from scratch. His Brunswick network was seventy miles away, so it offered limited help. To make things more difficult, Valoze told Ray that ATF was not interested in street-level crime this time—they wanted criminal organizations. How would you manage this, if you were Ray? You're in another new town and, once again, you know no one. You have limited English, no criminal knowledge to speak of, and your only way to stay with your family in the country you love is to serve up criminal organizations for the federal government. If you're Ray Khan, you start with what you know: the network of inner-city convenience store owners.

"Ray would meet most of the criminals through the cigarette business," Valoze recalls. "So, while he's doing his legitimate business, he's bringing us bad guys. He meets these people. He's driving around selling cigarettes and making contacts." This was where Ray thrived. Through his network in the tobacco trade, Ray was able to branch out and find people involved in high-level narcotics and firearms trafficking.

"He dealt with a lot of stores in the hood," Valoze says. "He would tell these gangsters about me (Sal) and my criminal enterprise, and he would bring them in to meet me. I would take it from there. The 'swag'—counterfeit clothing, electronics, jewelry, dick-hard pills, tobacco products, et cetera—at our warehouses would play a huge part in luring these criminal organizations and gangsters into our operation."

The agents say they had to give Ray legitimate merchandise which he could use to draw people in. "We had counterfeit goods, and legit stuff," Valoze says. "But when a bad guy walks into the warehouse and sees hundreds of cases of Nike sneakers, word on the street is you're a smuggler. They walk in and they're sold. He [Ray] had an import business, and the bad guys would see the props and then would ask about illegal imports. It was the greatest bait we could ever have—it was a distraction—the criminals seemed to care more about the swag than the business of selling guns and drugs."

On a day-to-day basis, Ray and the agents would hang around the warehouse, moving things around on forklifts to make their cover import-export business seem legitimate. Ray says he liked being on site, especially when he brought people in. While he wasn't always present for the deals they made with the agents, he felt some pride when people brought in illegal merchandise and sold it to the undercovers.

As with Ceasefire, the story was that Ray was the owner of the business. This also worked out well for the agents, as using Ray gave them an "out" if criminals proposed something which would violate ATF policy or procedure. "Ray wouldn't like that," or "Ray's not going to let us pay that much" became easy fallbacks which helped keep the mission on track.

Many of the Hispanic gangsters Ray brought in were obsessed with the electronics in the warehouse. The black customers wanted high-end clothing, and the white targets wanted cigarettes. Regardless of the demographic Ray introduced, they could all ship back this merchandise to their countries or communities for a huge profit. When they offered ridiculous trades, however, the agents would once again say Ray would never approve of the deal, which made it a lot easier when dealing with dangerous clientele.

Both Valoze and Lesnak remember a shipment of counterfeit sneakers they received to help with these undercover operations.

"The Al Pacino sneakers were the best," Lesnak says.

"These were knock-off Nikes with Tony Montana's face on them, a picture. Gangsters loved them. But they were the worst quality," Valoze laughs. "If you wore them, it was like wearing wood blocks on your feet. They had no support, and the bottom would come off because they weren't glued correctly. Like I said, all of the merchandise was worthless shit, but OIG tried to make a big deal out of that later, like we were doing something sinister or something. All of that counterfeit merchandise had been donated to a law-enforcement operation. Taxpayer money had not been used for any of it."

This was their "bait." If there were rodents or overly useless merchandise, "Lou Sir would take whole case and just—just throw them in the dumpster," Ray says. Here he is referring to palettes of outdated honey buns the warehouse received.

"There were only so many times you could move this stuff around," Valoze says. "After a while, the rats and roaches would just be too much, and we'd pitch them."

They couldn't have known it at the time, but these honey buns would become a huge point of contention in the future. "They're getting machine guns and drugs off the streets, but the Office of Inspector General only cared about the honey buns," Lesnak says. Again, though, we are getting ahead of ourselves here. At this point, Operation Crossbones was gaining traction, and Ray's cooperation was a huge reason.

As a federal agency, ATF was never really interested in diving deep into the world of untaxed cigarettes and money laundering (a field which is mostly dominated by HSI). They wanted gangs, guns, and drugs. With this focus in mind, Ray started bringing in some extremely violent people.

"Every deal seemed like it was gonna end in a gunfight," Valoze says, recalling the early days of the operation. Unlike the individuals they dealt with in the previous case, everyone Ray brought into Crossbones was a gang member, and they were all hostile and increasingly confrontational. Valoze recalls speaking with his team about how, with each new person Ray introduced, they felt like fists might start flying. Although it was increasingly dangerous, Valoze knew Ray was bringing in the right people: trigger-pullers, the people putting guns on the streets, and major drug dealers. Valoze had no idea how Ray met them, and even less clue about how he drew them into the undercover store where they ultimately met federal charges. Ray just did it.

"Sometimes, and this would happen a lot," Valoze says, "guys got so comfortable with us in there doing gun and dope deals, they would actually do other deals in there, like with other people, and we were like, uh-uh."

As with the previous operation, Ray was once more introduced as the owner, this time of Pulaski Distributors. Valoze says Ray wore this role like a badge of honor. It boosted his ego and fed into the way he treated people, which was often like shit. Regardless of his methods, though, his effectiveness was undeniable, and his results skyrocketed. Ray took his boss identity with him to the convenience stores he visited, building up his legitimate business while making the contacts the ATF wanted. Striking up relationships with the Indian store owners, Ray again was introduced to the gangbangers, bikers, and criminals who frequented the stores. At the same time, Ray and the undercover agents were pushing thousands of dollars in untaxed cigarettes every day, and they were moving product in Georgia and South Carolina.

"One time," Valoze says, "Ray was sent to retrieve money from a bad check given to them by a middle eastern target." In this case, Ray was asked to play the role of debt collector.

"You remember that one guy, Kenny," Ray asks Valoze. "He gave you bad check and you call me. It was bad check. Fifty thousand dollars, and Lou Sir call me and say, 'He gave it to us bad check fifty thousand dollars and we have to get this money.' And I say, 'No worry. I'll go over there.' And I go to the Macon and grab the money right away. I catch this guy. I just called him and told him, 'That's not the way to do business.' He already had orders for other things from warehouse. I had to play trick with him, saying that we couldn't get him any more stuff if he didn't pay the money."

"Yeah, he grabbed fucking cash from the guy and brought it to us." Valoze remembers Ray walking into the warehouse with fifty grand in a brown paper bag and a big smile on his face.

Valoze never knew what Ray had done to get that money back, but he sometimes felt safer not asking those kinds of questions.

"There were things Ray did outside of the undercover location that we preferred not to know about. And they never went into any official report," Valoze says.

Ray will tell you he never felt threatened, scared, or that he was in a dangerous situation. His quiet confidence is immeasurable. There was no doubt to Agent Valoze, or any of the undercovers Ray worked with, however, that Ray put himself in danger on a daily basis for their mission and to do what he thought was right.

The men recall a particular customer who frequented the warehouse, an old-school gangster who was arrested after the first phase of Operation Crossbones. He went by the name of Lincoln. Ray met this enterprising criminal as a fellow convenience-store owner who set up a store deep in Savannah's sketchiest ghetto.

"I went over to there and bad guys [Lincoln] talking to me like all kinds of stuff again like, 'You need this tomorrow or next day, like brick, whole brick [referring to a kilo of cocaine],' and next day he will take it over there. And then say, 'How about the fake money now? If you want to, I can bring samples tomorrow with the bricks and a couple of guns.' So, I tell the Lou Sir every morning, give the guy a call, and he can bring the cocaine bricks and guns together, and the fake money. But he was also a very cool guy. He's not like angry or anything, he always talks smooth and slowly…but he's big-time criminal."

Once again, Ray is reluctant to go too deeply into his methods. At times, it almost feels as though he is protecting the criminals he uncovered. It's clear, though, that he managed to create burgeoning friendships with a few of them, prior to turning them over to the feds.

"I found him [Lincoln] from the store. He used to own the store in the ghetto area. He used to own the store, and I go over there to sell the cigarettes. And that time I met him and to make the friendship with him and then I talking to him every day, like for ten days or like that, and then I start talking to him about drugs and guns and I told him to come to my warehouse. I have more stuff there, and then he start [doing business] with us."

At this point in the conversation Valoze realizes who Ray is talking about and tells him that Lincoln had confessed to "Sal" that he had killed five people.

"Oh, I didn't know that," Ray says, still unperturbed. "He speak slowly. Very silent. A good guy."

When the logical question is asked of him upon hearing about cases like this, Ray says he was never scared. He says he never got injured, even when people took him places in cars. "Never concerned, worried." Ray just smiles.

"The bigger the criminal the cooler they are," Valoze says. "The old gangsters are chill."

CHAPTER SIX

ATF agent Lou Valoze and Ray Khan had, over the years, developed a relationship which was beginning to move beyond the typical informant-handler's expectations. And it's clear this started during Operation Crossbones. Ray continued building his own business, while also working to bring every potential federal defendant he met to the warehouse. And the agents' operation was starting to look really promising. Everything seemed to be going the way Valoze hoped it would. At that time, however, Agent Valoze had not yet realized the depth of Billy Thompson's obsession with bringing down Ray Khan.

"Ray did keep fucking up," Valoze says. "But it was low-level shit, and on the other side, he was getting crime guns off the streets by the thousands."

Valoze is referring to Ray's continued sale of bootleg DVDs—white disks with movies illegally burned onto them and the titles scrawled onto the front of the discs in sharpie. "It's the 'little greed,'" Valoze says, which he claims is common among local businessmen in that part of the United States. "They can be millionaires, but there's always another dime to be made." Ray just smiles as he hears this from "Lou Sir," but he doesn't try to deny it.

In October of 2011, Ray brings in another new person to meet the ATF agents at the warehouse. Introducing himself as "Shawn," the young black male arrived at Crossbones just before 5:00 PM. He gave Valoze a baggie containing an off-white chunky substance, which later weighed 15.3 grams and tested positive for cocaine. When Valoze asked him whether he had any firearms he wanted to sell, only then did Shawn think to inquire: "Hey, you guys police?"

Valoze and his partners, of course, simply answered in the negative. Apparently, that was enough for Shawn, who pulled a handgun from his pants pocket, wiped off his fingerprints, and handed it to Valoze. When he asked what they were doing with the guns, Valoze gave the tried-and-true cover story.

"We take them to New York to resell," he stated, his northeastern accent selling the explanation. Most east-coast criminals are aware of New York's strict gun laws, and very few ever questioned this response. When Valoze showed Shawn hollowed-out pallets of merchandise where the guns were supposedly shipped, his story was sold. "Got any more of these?" Valoze asked, referring to the handgun.

Impressed by the operation, Shawn nodded. "Sure do."

Shawn sold Valoze a Cobra Enterprises .380 with a single magazine that day, and said he'd bring in more guns the next. When he asked Valoze how much the DVD players were, the agents gave him two to make up for a shortfall of funds they had available for the coke. This was how the business worked. And it worked very well. By August 15, 2011, Valoze's reports show, to that date, twenty individuals committed federal violations during the undercover transactions which occurred at the Crossbones warehouse. These violations included purchases of firearms from convicted felons, cocaine from local narcotics organizations, and CCTA (untaxed cigarette) transactions, some with illegals. By this date, the agents had also identified several money-laundering schemes.

Crossbones was picking up steam, and the criminals were sharing their own experiences at the warehouse. As always, however, the success of the investigation still relied on Ray getting out in the world to meet people like Shawn.

As part of Operation Crossbones, DOR had given him, as "Ray Khan," a license to sell cigarettes. Ray was doing well with this business and was looking to branch out. He had his eye on the slot-machine business, which was a profitable but highly regulated field, operated through licensure from the Department of Revenue and in affiliation with the Georgia State Lottery. Around this time, Ray recalls, Georgia capped the number of "master licenses" they issued, saying they did not intend to confer any more.

"Whoever has the license, that's it," Ray says. "No more. I know the gas-station people, but I don't have that license in order to put the machines in the businesses. So, I told the Lou Sir that I need that license."

It was time for Ray to flex a little and look towards his own future. Despite the Georgia ruling, ATF knew Ray's value to their operation and agreed to try and pull some strings for him.

"They talk to the DOR director and say, 'Ray needs the license.' And DOR director say, 'OK, come tomorrow and I give you the license.' So, they give me license, and after that I start my own business in my name with the machines. And I know the gas-station people everywhere. I talk to all these gas-station people, and put in three, four machine every day to all these gas-station people's stores."

It was here that Ray Khan's empire truly began. With the help of ATF, Ray managed the impossible: He was a master license holder. It was up to him, however, to grow this new business. Typically, he took the risks Ray is known for.

"That time I did not have so much money, so I borrow some money from some people to buy the machines that cost too much," Ray says. "And I try to make good relationships with the machine people, the company, so I tell them you give it to me, the credit, like four, five months, six months, but they just give me six months credit and I'm making the money off this machine. That's where I build my credit and everything from zero. I built a whole business."

Once again, Ray had taken out a hefty loan, but the very first thing he did was to work hard and he paid that loan off in well under the time allotted. A few years later, Ray also bought his house—what Valoze describes as a "mansion." At over seven thousand square feet, Valoze's description seems fair. It cost him several hundred thousand dollars, even in 2014. He paid that house off in less than two years. All while working as the most effective informant the ATF had ever seen. It's simply the way Ray does business. But back to Crossbones.

As the operation continued to grow and gain traction with local criminals, the undercover agents and their supervisors realized they were dealing with some extremely violent offenders. These criminals were still out in the community committing crimes and putting guns and drugs on the streets. Valoze says it simply wasn't right to leave them out there any longer.

"Eventually, we looked at who we had, and we decided that we need to take these people down," Valoze recalls. "Eventually, if these guys are out there killing people while we have charges on them that can get them off the streets, that's kind of on us. But we didn't want to shut the operation down because he [Ray] was just catching his wind."

Luckily, the warehouse Valoze had chosen for what became just the first phase of Operation Crossbones turned out to be the perfect choice. "This place was very remote," he says. "The warehouse was in a very remote, industrial location. But we were already into some very bad guys, so we asked, 'Can we just take down the worst of these guys? Can we take them down, no press releases, nothing, wall off the arrests and go to a totally different part of town, near the port, and keep this going? And we'll tell the other people we're dealing with that we're just going to a new location.' It happens all the time with businesses. It was a big undertaking. It had to happen very quietly."

The decision was made, and the agents were going to attempt something federal agencies are not necessarily trained for: the quietest takedown ever. Some of these early targets were people they hadn't dealt with for a long time, and many hadn't visited the warehouse in months. But Valoze left those details to his informant.

"Ray just called them back up and told them they had a truckload of stolen electronics, and we'll give you first looks," Valoze says. "And of course, Ray being Ray, he also told them that if they had any cocaine or guns to sell, bring that with you as well."

As Ray remembers, "I tried to organize, you know. Cause I'm the one bringing them, talking to these guys."

On January 25, 2012, the first takedown for Operation Crossbones went down—and that was where Ray got to play action hero.

"There was tons of action, man. It was insane," Valoze says. "And he got every single guy to show up. Some of them even showed up with other people, and they all had guns and cocaine, and we got a whole bunch of arrests out of that one."

Despite Ray's initial interference in their tactical planning, the SRT team which conducted the successful and very quiet takedown gave Ray a vest after everything happened.

"I still have that vest," he says with pride.

As a result of the first phase of Crossbones, and almost entirely due to Ray's contributions, twelve violent criminals were federally indicted, including Shawn, who had come to the warehouse several times and sold more drugs and firearms to the agents. On June 5, 2012, Shawn pleaded guilty to those charges in federal court. He was sentenced five months later to fifteen years in prison and five years of supervised probation. It was just another example of one more dangerous felon Ray had gotten off the streets of Savannah.

He also managed to keep the operation's other suspects on the hook as Crossbones transitioned to its second, and much more ambitious, phase.

***

While ATF couldn't publicize this first takedown, it was still celebrated internally. What the higher-ups didn't appreciate, while they patted each other's backs and congratulated each other on another successful operation, was that Agent Valoze, many of his undercover team members, and, more importantly, their informant all actually lived in the community where Operation Crossbones took place.

"Ray knows at this point that an armed gang of local drug dealers suspect they've been infiltrated because of him. Does he leave town? No," ATF agent Lesnak says. "Until those guys are arrested, he's in as much risk as Lou is. They live down the street."

This is the real danger when it comes to being a confidential informant. While your agents stay behind their counters, in their warehouse, constantly monitored by cameras and protected by a security team, you are out on the streets. The streets where you live. The streets where your family lives. As he became responsible for the arrests of more and more violent felons, however, Valoze will tell you Ray just seemed empowered.

"We owe Lou and Ray a sense of loyalty for what they did and how they did it," Lesnak says, shaking his head as the men reminisce about their time in Savannah. "When they [informants] get uncovered, they lose all prospect of working for legitimate *and* criminal organizations." But this didn't faze Ray Khan. He was never going to work for anyone but Ray Khan again, so what did that matter to him?

It was clear to Valoze, as well as everyone else they worked with, that Ray was just getting started and they were all excited to see just how far his involvement could take them. They needed to get Crossbones up and running again, and they needed to do it fast. Part of these types of operations is word of mouth, and the other is momentum. The longer they were out of business, the more impetus they lost. It took a while, but Valoze knew that with Ray's help, they had a lot more felons to take down.

After the first phase, Operation Crossbones was moved to Garden City, near the Port of Savannah. Established as a way to house industrial and agricultural workers employed in the larger town of Savannah, Garden City sits at the east end of Route 80 and boasts a host of port- and rail-based industry. In 2010, the town had around ten thousand inhabitants, about 80 percent of whom were a balanced mix of black and white. The cover location for the new business was to be located at the entrance of the Port of Savannah, which had been mostly overlooked in previous federal investigations, despite the volume of land-and-sea-based trade it supported. It took over a year to create the import-export business backdrop for this second phase, and to complete the physical wiring of microphones, cameras, safe rooms, and equipment monitoring rooms, but Agent Valoze will tell you it was perfect.

While the logistics of the new business location were being handled, the undercover agents were kept busy. They maintained contact with suspects from the first phase of Crossbones who were unaware of the ATF takedown while they created the infrastructure of their undercover personae: bank accounts, internet and cable accounts, permits, licenses, vehicle registrations, house rental, and so on. The same was true of Ray, who was now working for ATF Agent Tom Lesnak as well, who continued to provide the backing for Ray to sell legitimate, stamped cigarettes. This would allow him to make a living, while also keeping him on the road and making contacts in preparation for the next level of the investigation. Once again, Agent Tom Lesnak continued providing Operation Crossbones with much of the counterfeited merchandise Ray used to build the operation's freight-forwarding company cover story.

As the preparations for phase two of Crossbones continued, Agent Valoze was completing yet more immigration-related paperwork to try to keep Ray in the country. In one such application, dated April 17, 2012, Valoze writes, "Due to his background and experience in the tobacco and retail business, the alien has the unique ability to interact with individuals involved in the criminal aspect of these businesses, and introduce them to undercover agents."

Valoze says to this day there has never been an informant as productive as Ray Khan. In fact, at the time Valoze wrote this recommendation to the immigration service on Ray's behalf, Ray was assisting on numerous cases with ATF, the Savannah Police Department, and, ironically, the Georgia Department of Revenue and ICE. Through his networks, which dug their roots into the Indian-based businesses around Savannah, Ray was bringing money laundering, narcotics, gang-based, and a variety of other investigations to all these agencies in the surrounding area. Even outside of ATF, Ray Khan's prowess as a confidential informant was becoming well known.

"The East Indian community is tough to infiltrate," says former ATF Agent Tom Lesnak. "It's a closed community. It's why you don't see many cases against these tight communities."

In making these observations, it is clear Lesnak recognizes the value of identifying the best informant for each operation. "We all had a role—I can't play certain types," Lesnak continues. "I had my role as a guy who ran a successful company." And they would send Ray into the convenience stores, the gas stations, and, once his master license had been approved, the slot machine halls.

"Guys like Ray were the ones who would bring in the real bad guys," Lesnak finishes. It's what Ray had been able to do in the past, and Operation Crossbones once again demanded that Ray somehow manage to up his game yet further.

Another of Valoze's endorsements of Ray highlights the importance of his role: "The alien's cooperation with the government consists of the alien introducing targets to the undercover agents for the purpose of the agents' infiltration of these targets and organizations. Due to his experience in the industry, he has the ability to interact with individuals and criminal organizations, lending an air of authenticity to undercover agents' eventual contact with the targets. The alien has been successful in arranging for these targets to meet with undercover agents at the undercover location."

It became an important detail for both Valoze and Ray that the application was signed by Agent Valoze's superior officer without ever being returned to him for corrections, omissions, or concerns. Ultimately, ATF, with support from the Southern Georgia US Attorney's Office, began the process for an S-visa (often referred to as a "snitch visa") on Ray's behalf.

Even as multi-year federal prison sentences for those indicted in Operation Ceasefire began rolling in, Ray's status in the United States was, at best, shaky. While the government's wheels ground slowly through the process, Valoze was keeping Ray in the country on a month-by-month basis. Ray's dedication to Agent Valoze and the Operation Crossbones mission, however, remained steadfast, and as soon as the new warehouse site opened, Ray started bringing in criminal organizations from all walks of life.

What neither Ray nor Agent Valoze realized at this time was that the assistant US attorney (AUSA) they were working with could have worked to remove the deportation from his record.

"But no one know about that," says Ray.

Had this happened, however, Ray's story could have been significantly changed. As it was, Ray went back to what always worked for him.

"I met many of those people in South Carolina outside the gas station there," he says. When asked for more details, Ray is always reticent. Just how did he draw people to come and meet with federal agents away from these meeting spots?

"Because suddenly, if they come to the warehouse to see Lou Sir and Ralf and Brian and the other agents, they might be going to think, 'Yeah, they might be police.' But I am talking to them every day for five times and tell them, 'They are my guys, man, don't worry. No problem, man.' So, they can believe that and then, slowly, slowly, they started to do the deals all the time with us."

One of the organizations Ray befriended and brought to the warehouse to meet Valoze and his crew was a predominantly Hispanic organization operating out of South Carolina, Florida, and New York. They were actively involved in the trafficking of stolen vehicles, narcotics, and firearms. One day, when Ray was at the warehouse working with agents, one of the members of this group arrived. Known to them initially as Paolo, Ray met this man through connections he had made at one of his friends' convenience stores in South Carolina, just on the border with Georgia. After speaking to Ray a few times at that location, Paolo agreed to come to the warehouse to be introduced to Sal.

Through a mix of Agent Valoze's Spanish and Paolo's broken English, he told them he could get kilos of coke for $22,000 from a Mexican in Savannah. He also told them he could get similar weight from contacts in Atlanta. Paolo goes on to tell Valoze he sells the kilos for $30,000–$32,000. It seemed like an easy deal for Valoze, until Paolo broke the news that he and Valoze could each make $500 if they could forward the money for the brick. Valoze had played that game before, and he wasn't about to hand tens of thousands over to Paolo, a guy he'd just met. He learned that lesson the hard way and only just got away with it the first time.

Valoze told Paolo he'd let him know, already knowing he had no intention of fronting the money. Unfortunately, this was often the way with drug dealers. They'd talk a big game, but when it came down to getting the deal done, they weren't reliable or as flush with cash as they'd made it seem. It didn't hurt Valoze's feelings, but he could tell it always disappointed Ray.

Ever the businessman, however, Ray maintained his demeanor while Paolo looked around the warehouse. It turns out that he was likely assessing the operation and the agents he'd just met. After walking around for a while, Paolo came back to where Ray and Agent Valoze were chatting behind the counter.

"You wanna buy some coke now?" he asked, pulling a bag from his left pocket. While it wasn't a kilo, Valoze did end up buying 1.2 oz. of cocaine from Paolo, thereby ensuring his later indictment. He thought that might be the last they'd see of Paolo and the last they'd hear of his big talk, but no one was more surprised than Valoze when he showed back up at the warehouse a few weeks later.

"They asking for thirty thousand," Ray says of the brick of cocaine Paolo brought in. "We bargaining with them and we check everything and they just give us a deal."

After some serious negotiations and when he threw in several cartons of untaxed cigarettes to sweeten the deal, the agents paid $18,000 for a brick of the best cocaine Valoze had ever seen.

Ray's safety was a constant concern for his controlling agents, but there was little they could do to protect him when he was away from the warehouse. When he came across a group of car thieves, Ray says he even ended up going to Virginia with them.

"I go with them everywhere," he says as Valoze shakes his head in disbelief. "They show me the back of a warehouse and say, 'Here we change the car numbers and use a salvage plate,' or something like that. I don't ask them too much, but I saw everything. So, they like, they feel like best friends. And I talk to them all kinds of stuff, so they just suddenly say, they going to bring forty or fifty AK-47s, fully automatic."

How the man is even alive is a miracle. You can see it in Valoze's eyes as he hears the stories. When he asks Ray how he's invited on these little filed trips, Ray offers his customary shrug.

"They are like friends to me," he says when pressed. "Plus, they feel like they want to do business with us."

And they came through with the firearms.

"They were machine guns. Fully automatic," Valoze recalls. "It's an ATF agent's wet dream. They're gun traffickers and they're operating a stolen car ring. And we found out the FBI is working this stolen car ring, and we were able to work the whole case, indict, and arrest them all under the FBI's nose. It was one of the greatest moments of my career."

Another gun purchase with this group involved twenty-five fully automatic AK-47s with the serial numbers removed and ten .50 caliber handguns.

"These were just more dangerous firearms that Ray was helping to get off the streets," says Valoze.

While these huge investigations were being carried out by all of the agents involved in the operation, Ray Khan continued bringing in more suspects to the warehouse. Despite the fact that some were talking to him about recent takedowns in the area, Ray regularly delivered convicted felons who sold the agents guns and drugs. Many of these transactions didn't even involve giving the bad guys money. The agents had a warehouse full of flat-screen TVs provided from seizures in other cases, and they would use these as trades to get guns and drugs off the streets. It was rewarding work, but as the months grounded on, the agents felt the pressure.

"Bad guys work hard," Lesnak says, remembering the endless hours he put into his own long-term investigations. "The real crooks don't stop working at five o'clock. We worked every day, and the bad guys recognized that."

There is nothing convenient about being an undercover ATF agent. Valoze and his team were away from their families for weeks at a time, sometimes longer. Lesnak and Valoze commiserate with each other as they remember missed birthday parties for their kids and anniversaries with their wives. While they would certainly hesitate to admit they'd do it all again at this point in their reminiscences, at the time they felt their dedication to these cases was necessary.

"The guys who were successful were the guys who were willing to work," Lesnak says. "It's not a Monday to Friday thing."

The same was true for Ray. At this point, his own business was finally beginning to gain traction. This meant he needed to put in the time, of course, all while he also felt the pressure to keep performing for Operation Crossbones. It was a balance, and on one side of the scale was his ever-tenuous immigration status.

Ray is not afraid of hard work and long hours, though, and language barriers were also not a deterrent for him. Being a non-native English speaker, Ray is used to working harder than most to get his point across. A mere language barrier wasn't going to stand in his way and, as the operation continued, Ray found himself in with some Mexican cartel members who were running dope through Georgia. He then started bringing Mexican cartel members into the warehouse. How does this happen? How does a normal business guy who is just selling cigarettes across the state run into cartel members?

"I always go to everybody gas station," he says. "I go to a friend's gas station and talking to my friends and all and see what customer comes, and what kind of bad guys, and then I go outside and I'm talking to these people."

It's that easy. Well, they all need fuel. Runners need to gas up their cars, and they'll hit the low-end places with fewer cameras when they are available. And Ray knows that guy, the owner of that independent liquor store or convenience store, and then he just does his magic. Talking with them as they came through buying fuel, Ray somehow managed to work his way into their confidence.

"Those Mexicans live in those trailer in park [trailer parks]," he says. "Yeah, those people live over there. . . ."

"He would go there, into those fucking trailer parks," Valoze interjects.

"How I met them," Ray goes on, "I was at one of my friend's gas stations and then they come over there. Then I talking to them and then they take me to the trailer and show me the gun, drugs, and all. I say come tomorrow to my warehouse and I can show you TVs."

This was how Ray bridged the gaps. To find the right people, Ray showed them counterfeit items, including electronics. TVs, DVD players, and tablets. He piled them into his van, alongside his cigarettes, and showed them around until he met the people the agents wanted. And then, of course, Ray put himself in danger.

"And then I go to those Mexican people, exchange the number, and they call me to come to trailer," he says. "And I go to them's trailer and then behind the trailer, they take me to the woods, and they show me a lot of guns."

When pressed for details, the story gets more frightening. Picture yourself in the dark, in woods behind the trailer of some Mexican cartel members you met at a gas station. They lead you further and further into the darkness. You're stumbling over fallen branches as the smell of wet leaves fills your nose. Further you go, away from the lights of the trailer park. You showed these guys some cheap TVs; do they think you're rich enough to kidnap? To hold for ransom?

"These are cartel guys," Valoze says. "And a lot of them really don't speak shit for English."

In truth, Ray has no clue where he's going or why. And then these Mexican guys each grab a shovel, and they start digging. What would you do? Run? Pass out? Start calling for help? If you're Ray, you fall back on your new friendships with the men, your general faith in humanity despite all you've been though, and you wait to see what they are doing.

"There inside the woods, you know," Ray says, "they digging the stuff and pulling out bags and it look like all nothing. And one of those guys, Mark…M…I don't remember. He giving to us a lots of good bricks, very good bricks. You always say [Ray looks at Valoze], 'That's the bricks I never see like that.'"

Buried in the woods behind the trailer parks, these cartel members had bricks of cocaine, stashes of firearms, and pounds upon pounds of methamphetamine.

"This was the beginning of the super labs in Mexico," says Valoze. "And now they are selling us meth and it's ninety-nine percent pure. In the early 2000s I'm buying meth, and it was dirty, and really low quality, and now this is where we start seeing this shit and it's pure."

One problem when dealing with cartel members, particularly those from south of the US borders, is identifying them. Most are in the country illegally and have no form of American identification. As they continued dealing with these men, the ATF agents became increasingly frustrated when trying to identify them. They were coming up empty. In order to indict and then arrest them, they needed a good ID. In comes Ray Khan. As they deal with the group more often, Valoze identifies the highest in the chain and points him out to Ray.

"I need you to find out who that one is," he says when the group visits the store. Valoze nods towards the leader of the group.

"Yes sir, Lou Sir," is Ray's response.

After a few more days have passed, Ray contacts the cartel again and asks the leader if he wanted a cut of the business Ray is bringing in. All Ray would want in exchange is a good price on the meth the agents are already buying. When the man agrees, Ray takes him to his warehouse so he can add him as his "agent." Of course, Ray somehow convinces the man that in order to pay him, he needs his ID. The cartel member delivered his passport to the ATF himself.

Once again, Ray and the undercover ATF agents spent much of their time, when they weren't buying contraband, moving pallets and crates of merchandise around the warehouse. It needed to appear as if the site was an active import-export business, so this movement kept it looking fresh for repeat visitors. One such visitor was "Javier," who was, of course, introduced to Agent Valoze by Ray Khan.

From July 2012 through January 2013, Agent Valoze bought sixteen firearms from Javier, his family, and other gangsters Javier introduced to the undercover agents—mostly in exchange for televisions. Several of these firearms were stolen, and many were crime guns. During their interactions with Javier, he told Agent Valoze that his uncle, Martin, was another very dangerous Mexican cartel member. When the ATF agents identified the man as Martin García Rodriguez, they found out he was indeed a notorious cartel member—one engaged in kidnapping…and likely much more. Thinking he was being kind, Javier told them he didn't want to bring Martin to the warehouse as he was afraid of him coming back to burglarize the warehouse and stealing all their merchandise.

Javier's attempt at kindness was not, however, matched by any good sense. On May 13, 2013, Javier called Agent Valoze to tell him he had several firearms he wanted to trade for a large flat-screen television. On this occasion, however, he brought his five-year-old son, "Pancho," to the deal. Javier seriously brought his kid, a Smith & Wesson .44 Magnum revolver, a Hermann Weihrauch .32 caliber revolver, and a Henry Repeating Arms .22 caliber rifle, which was loaded with two rounds, to this deal with—as far as Javier was concerned—known criminals. The agents were disgusted. While another agent kept the child outside the deal room, Agent Valoze laid into Javier. Needless to say, it was made clear that he was never to bring the child to the warehouse again. When all was said and done, "Javier" was sentenced to seventy months of federal prison, followed by deportation from the United States.

When the takedown for the second phase of Operation Crossbones occurred on June 18, 2013, the press release compiled by the Department of Justice states "undercover ATF agents purchased guns and drugs from multiple criminal organizations whose scope ranged from regional to international. The undercover agents were able to infiltrate these organizations over a period of time, ultimately purchasing 189 firearms, including handguns, assault rifles, sawed-off shotguns and machine guns; illegal drugs, including over 200 grams of heroin and more than 4 kilograms of cocaine; and stolen vehicles."[2] Thirty-three more defendants were charged with firearms, narcotics, and other federal offenses. The vast majority of these charges came as a result of Ray's introductions.

Despite his stellar work with the ATF, Ray Khan—whose cooperation was never recognized by ATF or any of Agent Valoze's chain of command—was barely scraping by financially by selling cigarettes. His slot-machine empire was starting to grow, but it was a slow beginning, and it would still be a few years before Ray bought that big house.

Although he was unable to assist him directly with his financial concerns, Agent Valoze did not abandon Ray after Crossbones was finished. Every thirty days, paperwork was filed for Ray requesting the extension of his legal status in the US, and in September of 2013, Ray assisted law enforcement with the identification and arrest of another large-scale criminal enterprise. On this occasion, Ray utilized his unique gifts to convince a prolific money launderer to open his vault, capturing on camera what Valoze remembers as "boatloads of cash."

"This was Ray at his best," Valoze says. "The other stuff was just vindictive bullshit."

Here Valoze is referring to Ray's next arrest—another Thompson-driven investigation which resulted in Ray being

---

2 United States Attorney's Office Southern District of Georgia. "45 Defendants Charged On Gun, Drug Trafficking And Related Offenses Following Undercover Investigation." *Department of Justice*. June 19, 2013. Accessed August 10, 2025. https://www.justice.gov/usao-sdga/pr/45-defendants-charged-gun-drug-trafficking-and-related-offenses-following-undercover

charged for putting a video poker machine which paid out cash in one of his stores.

"It was just one more battle to keep Ray out of jail and working for me," says Agent Valoze, though his support for his strange, yet effective, informant never waned during this time or at any time after. "What most people won't realize is that Ray was never paid a dime for his work as a confidential informant," Valoze says. "Helping him get a license for those slot machines was the absolute least we could do."

While Ray dealt with the locals, defendants from Crossbones were going through the courts, receiving decades in federal time. True to form, the ATF and US Attorney's Office basked in the recognition of their contributions, but Ray still had to rely on the support of Valoze and his ATF chain of command to remain in the US. Further trouble for Ray would erupt alongside volleys of complaints between the local police agencies from Crossbones and the ATF agents involved.

CHAPTER SEVEN

If you read any true crime book detailing the lives of undercover federal agents, you will learn about the tolls this type of work takes on not only the agents, but also on their families. By this time in his career, ATF Agent Lou Valoze turned and burned four long-term undercover operations in a row, and the cracks in his world were showing. His wife and children lived without Valoze's consistent presence in their lives for years. He missed special occasions, but also the small moments which mean so much when your kids are young: the first days of school and graduations, family trips to visit his wife's relatives in New York, and weekends away. These were times Valoze would never get back.

In truth, Valoze realizes with hindsight that he consciously distanced himself while he was so deeply invested in his cases. His family lived too close to these investigations for comfort. He couldn't bear the thought of tracking the figurative dirt which came with undercover work into his family home. However, despite being surrounded by agents and other supporting staff,

Valoze was lonely. As a result, and as so frequently happens when immersed in long-term investigations like these, he entered into an ill-advised affair with one of the federal prosecutors who worked on his cases. They had done well to keep the relationship quiet over the years, but these things have a habit of showing up at the worst possible times, and Valoze's luck had almost expired. For now, however, his indiscretion remained a secret which plagued only his own conscience.

Ray, meanwhile, was slowly building an empire. He remarried, and his slot machines were showing up in convenience stores and gas stations across Georgia. He accepted a plea regarding the video poker machine, unable to fight the charge when the machine obviously paid out cash winnings to players. This was against the law—a fact Ray will argue, of course.

Valoze and Ray saw each other less frequently during the downtime between operations. Each man was absorbed in their own work, their own life. Valoze was trying to reintegrate into his family, a difficult undertaking which was similar to the detachment and disconnect that soldiers face when returning from deployment. The cases now required paperwork and court appearances, which meant facing people Valoze lied to during the entire operation. Despite knowing he was on the right side of these meetings, he still felt an unexplained guilt when looking into the eyes of some of the defendants. It plagues him to this day. However, he took the brunt of this so Ray could avoid being put into that situation.

In one appearance during a trial for Crossbones, Valoze was asked how he had met the defendant, and he told the court he was introduced by an informant. The next question came from the US attorney—yes, the one who Valoze was sleeping with:

"What was the reason that this informant was working as an informant? What benefit would he receive?"

To this, Valoze replied, "He received status in this country. To be here legally is the benefit that he receives."

While it had almost nothing to do with the prosecution of the defendant who requested this hearing, this ostensibly innocuous exchange between Valoze and the federal prosecutor would later be examined in minute detail. And all of it would ultimately affect Ray Khan.

Meanwhile, Ray's participation in federal investigations continued. While he wasn't working with Valoze, Ray's renown had other agents requesting him to help with their cases.

"We pimped him out," former ATF agent Lesnak says. "We whored him out to whoever would use him. To keep him working."

Lesnak says he felt like a travel agent at times, moving informants around the country to help with different cases. In 2013, a former ATF agent who was working as an investigator for a private tobacco company in Los Angeles contacted him about a large-scale cigarette counterfeiting case, and Lesnak knew just the guy to help.

The tobacco company paid to fly Ray to California, and he got right to work. Over the course of this operation, Ray infiltrated a group of Chinese smugglers who were importing counterfeit Marlboro cigarettes to the United States. No, Ray doesn't speak Chinese, and yes, Chinese nationals are among the hardest, most-closed off groups to investigate. But this is Ray Khan we're talking about. More about this investigation later. What is important right now is that Ray's value was recognized nationwide. He was working with ATF and HSI and assisting in corporate investigations. It was an exciting time to be Ray Khan. His confidence was at an all-time high, which is impressive as

Ray doesn't lack self-esteem at the best of times. And still, he would continue to amaze his handlers.

Despite the mental toll which follows any long-term investigation, and the family-related issues Agent Valoze was dealing with in his personal life, he was once again looking for his next case. "Gideon" operations were some of the most successful undercover operations ever conducted by ATF or any other federal agency. They were the brainchild of ATF Special Agent Richie Zayas, who worked out of field offices in South Florida. Richie, who, like Agent Valoze, was a member of the ATF Enhanced Undercover Program, would conduct these operations in different cities throughout the country. Each of the cities targeted for a Gideon operation was experiencing record levels of gun-and-narcotics-related crime. This was Agent Valoze's wheelhouse.

At the start of each Gideon operation, Richie would assemble about twenty to thirty undercover agents, support staff, and as many confidential informants as he could round up. He would bring these people in early so support personnel could get set up and the informants could be pushed out onto the streets to start making connections with the gun traffickers, narcotics traffickers, and gang members. The agents would come in soon after. The informants would then start funneling the bad guys to the undercovers so they could initiate gun and drug transactions. Essentially, ATF would saturate the crime-ridden areas of a city for a period of time and go after the trigger-pullers, the violent gang members, and the criminals who were putting guns and dangerous drugs on the streets.

The courts and the media would eventually go sideways on ATF's Gideon operations, just as they did with the Storefront operations, claiming that they unfairly targeted minorities and used questionable tactics. No one ever argued that these types of operations failed to drastically reduce violent crime in these communities, because the results spoke for themselves. In 2014, after the conclusion of Operation Crossbones, Zayas recruited Agent Valoze to participate in a Gideon operation in Cleveland. Zayas had helped Agent Valoze by doing some undercover work in both Operation Ceasefire and Crossbones, and he had met Ray Khan and seen him work during those operations. Zayas asked Valoze to bring Ray with him, so Valoze reached out to Ray to see if he was interested.

"Hey, Ray. Do you want to come to Cleveland with me to help out in a big undercover operation?"

"Sir, what would I have to do?"

"Just go out, find bad guys, and bring them to me." Valoze knew this was Ray's talent, and he had confidence his CI would continue to produce, even in yet another new city.

"Sir, let's go to Cleveland." It was as easy as that for Ray when it came to requests from Valoze. His loyalties were set in stone.

Several days later, Ray and Valoze were on a plane to Ohio and settled into their hotel rooms. They would get to work the next day. Valoze got Ray into a fancy rental car and turned him loose on the streets of Cleveland. This was the way Ray liked it. He'd hit the streets on his own and work his magic. He would visit the gas stations in target neighborhoods and introduce himself to the owners, who were mostly Indian Americans in this part of the country. This was how he networked in the South, and it worked the same way in Cleveland. He knew what questions to ask, and he watched the interactions the owners had with the locals. He knew how to unearth the players and how to identify the dangerous criminals. Most importantly, somehow, he was always able to get introduced to these individuals. He got in with these guys at the street level and worked his way up. This was Ray's unique talent.

And it wasn't just common street thugs he could bring in. Ray was able to network his way into home invasion crews, cartels, money-laundering operations, and in Cleveland, even the Italian Mafia. On his second day in Cleveland, Ray called Agent Valoze. At this point in their working friendship, Valoze believed Ray couldn't surprise him anymore. He was wrong.

"Sir, have you heard of the Gambinos?" he asked.

"Are you talking about the famous Italian Mafia family?"

"Yes, sir," Ray said. "That is them."

"Of course I've heard of them. What about them?"

"I have met two of them and they want to meet with us to discuss buying untaxed cigarettes from us."

"Are you fuckin' kidding me?"

"No, sir."

Ray had certainly gotten to work right away. Through discussions with some of the Indian store owners, he was told there were several Italians in the neighborhood who were also interested in obtaining cases of cigarettes at bargain-basement prices. Ray convinced one of the store owners to introduce him to the Italians, people he was told were members of the Gambino crime family. Somehow, Ray had managed to get an introduction to two of these gangsters that night.

Obviously, Ray dealt with members of several different types of gangs and criminal enterprises at this point in time. His first interaction with one, however, had come when he was a college student in India. When he started school at C. U. Shah University in Surendranagar, India, Ray quickly became aware of a large group of young men who were terrorizing students on the campus.

“They were trying to rule the campus,” Ray says.

One day, when Ray arrived at school, he was confronted by some members of this gang as he was parking his car.

“You can’t park here,” he was told. When he hesitated to move his car from the prime parking spot he’d been lucky to find, a hand came down hard on the hood.

“Move!” he was ordered.

Ray was no stranger to the criminal element. Being a police officer in India is a dangerous job. Although his father didn’t talk much about his work, there were times it trickled through his barriers. Ray could see some other gang members walking towards his car. He started the engine and moved, parking further from the campus but avoiding immediate confrontation. His father might have approved, but he’d also know his son wasn’t going to let the incident slide completely. Ray was street smart. He needed to devise a plan.

“The principal is scared of those guys,” Ray says. “They rule the college.” At this private college, the governing body were ill-equipped to deal with any on-campus violence, let alone a full-blown gang incursion.

Ray wasn’t scared, though. We know Ray better than that.

“I had four or five friends, very strong like me. Like an Indian gang,” Ray remembers. “Around four o’clock, school is done, I came down from the classes and I saw that guy, and I told him, ‘You told me to park over there,’ and I suddenly grabbed his head, and I keep beating him.” Ray recreates the act as he tells the story, his fist punching towards the imagined head he held in his hands.

“He has four or five other guys,” Ray continues, “and they try to come at me. But my guys come with the hockey sticks and baseball bats. They just beat them up very bad, all of them.”

His smile breaks through as he recalls his physical prowess. Right or wrong, Ray Khan is still proud of himself to this day.

"We told them get out and they said they would come back with a lot of people, and I just call my dad," Ray finishes. "He sent like twenty, thirty police over there and these police they just beat them up very bad. And he told those bosses that if they come, he will beat them, too."

Clearly things work differently in India. Or maybe Ray is just more direct than we are used to when hearing about such matters.

As a result of this act, Ray earned the gratitude of the principal and the respect of his peers. He went on to hold the general secretary position (similar to student president in the US) in the college for all three years of his degree. Never once will Ray ever admit to being scared. Not when surrounded by lower caste members out for blood, and not even when confronted with gang members holding a college campus for ransom. And now, Ray was playing with the big boys: the Italian Mafia.

"I had Lou Sir a meeting with that guy," Ray says. It took him just two days to make contact with them. How had he found them? How had this ever happened?

"Just talking to the people and just making meeting," Ray says, when pushed to reveal his methods. "I forget who I talk to. His family was like Italian cartel. I know that's some kind of bad guy, but I don't know."

Valoze elaborates a little on Ray's explanations. "Because Indian people own so many businesses in the hood, there's a little alliance between them," he says. Ray had used these connections to find criminals, though he had no idea who they were.

"I go everywhere to like talking with people," Ray says. "I saw a couple of guys, and I thought that must be ATF, those are not bad guys."

The mobsters were too well dressed, Ray believed, to be criminals. In his limited experience with organized crime groups, Ray dealt mostly with street gangs. He didn't believe these well-dressed Italians could be gangsters. He thought they had to be undercover agents pretending to be criminals.

In another new town, an unfamiliar environment, Ray used his tried-and-true tactics: "I just go outside of gas station and talk to them. Literally in the ghetto. Everywhere has bad guys. People come and talk, like black people see Indian guys and they are talking as they think we are the owner." Apparently, this also worked for the Italian Mafia.

Once he had been introduced, Ray then convinced these new acquaintances that he and his partner had unlimited access to untaxed cigarettes coming out of the south, and that they could arrange to have them delivered to them in Cleveland. Ray played to his real strengths when he was talking about cigarette trafficking. He set up the meeting for the following night in downtown Cleveland, telling them that his partner was American and would be able to communicate with them better. Ray was always good at pretending that his English was not so good when it suited him.

As with the previous operations, cigarette trafficking was very low on ATF's list of priorities in Cleveland. ATF is supposed to concentrate their efforts on combating gangs, illegal guns, and drugs. However, although ATF does not regulate the tobacco industry, they are still responsible for enforcing the federal cigarette-trafficking laws. It's a little-known fact that organized crime groups, like the Italian Mafia, Colombian drug cartels, motorcycle gangs, Eastern European gangs, and terrorist organizations like Hezbollah and Hamas all engage in cigarette trafficking at some level to fund their activities. These organizations know it is a high-reward crime (huge profits) with little risk (resulting in light sentences with little to no jail time, if convicted).

When Agent Valoze told Zayas that he was meeting with two members of the Gambino crime family the next day to discuss assisting them in a cigarette-trafficking operation, Zayas didn't know what to say. Valoze explained Ray found these guys and set up the meeting at a restaurant. Ray had even written down the license plate of the Lincoln Navigator that one of the gangsters was driving, which enabled ATF to run the plate. It was short work to determine that the registered owner was indeed a made member of the Gambino crime family.

The next day, with a cover team stationed in the parking lot and electronic surveillance equipment on Agent Valoze's person, Ray and Agent Valoze met with the two gangsters at the restaurant. The men looked like they came right out of central casting for a mafia movie. The vast majority of times when Ray would introduce Agent Valoze to criminals, Valoze would take over the conversation, because Ray couldn't really talk in depth about guns, drugs, and gangster shit. But when it came to cigarette trafficking and tax evasion, Ray was a subject matter expert. So, this time Agent Valoze sat back and let Ray work his magic. Ray briefly explained how they were able to obtain master cases of cigarettes without tax stamps, but didn't give the gangsters too much information. Agent Valoze cut in to add that, in order for them to deliver the cases of cigarettes to them in Cleveland, it was he and Ray who would be taking all the risks. That, of course, would be an additional cost. It would be worth it, however, because of the drastically reduced price of the untaxed cigarettes.

The gangsters appeared to like what they were hearing. Ray and Agent Valoze had been in the cigarette-trafficking game for years and knew what they were talking about. Agent Valoze decided they should quit while they were ahead and told the gangsters he wanted to set up another meeting in a few days, so he could provide them with the exact pricing for the brands they wanted to order. The bigger of the two gangsters told Valoze they would contact him the next day with the meeting spot. Ray and Valoze excused themselves, stood up, and left the restaurant.

Adrenaline coursed through Valoze as he walked away. The. Freaking. Gambino. Family. He'd just sat at a table with Italian Mafia members. It was a federal agent's dream case, and it was once again due to his unlikely informant. While Valoze wrestled with his excitement and self-control, however, Ray seemed unaffected. Whether he truly understood the scope of what he had accomplished was debatable. Regardless, Ray remained calm and, apparently, unaffected.

Two days later Ray and Agent Valoze found themselves meeting with the same two gangsters at a coffee shop in Cleveland. Once again, there was a cover team set up nearby and Valoze was wearing a bug. As they probed for details, the smaller gangster asked more questions about the operation down south. Agent Valoze could tell they were still feeling them out and trying to gather more information. When you're a made member of an organized crime group, the last thing you want to do is bring in someone unvetted and who turns out to be a snitch or an undercover. Little did these men know, they were dealing with both. Ray and Valoze answered all his questions without offering up too much extra information. Valoze explained they had been operating in Georgia and the Carolinas for years (which was true), and that they wanted to expand their business northward. It made sense to the gangsters, who recognized the value of a business of this type, and seemed to appreciate the organization Ray and Valoze described.

The meeting was going well and Agent Valoze decided to pose the question. "So, are you guys ready to start talking about prices and quantity for an initial order?"

The gangsters looked at each other and the smaller one replied. "We're gonna run it by our people and, if everything checks out, we'll be placing an order by the end of the week." They were in.

Valoze learned from experience not to push his luck with these types of meetings. He told the gangsters he and Ray were looking forward to hearing from them, shook their hands, and left the coffee shop. Once again, Valoze and Ray were feeling pretty good about themselves and the potential of this operation. Unbeknownst to Agent Valoze, however, that meeting would be the last time he would ever work in an undercover capacity again, and the last time he would ever work with Ray.

Early the next morning, Valoze received numerous phone calls. Bad things were quickly developing back in Georgia. An Operation Crossbones task force officer had been accused of stealing flat-screen televisions from the operation and, to make things worse, these accusations were also tied to the chief of police in Savannah. Claims of wrongdoing started flying, and ATF Internal Affairs and the FBI had already been called in to investigate. As much as he hated to do it, Valoze told Agent Zayas about the situation and explained he didn't want any of this potential trouble to taint the new Cleveland operation. With his heart heavy with disappointment, Agent Valoze told Zayas he and Ray were going to catch the first flight back to Savannah.

On the way, Agent Valoze started hearing more details about the accusations his operation was facing. And it wasn't good. At the height of the Crossbones case, Valoze recalled he had been approached by one of the trainee agents who was assisting on the operation.

"Did any of you guys come in last night? 'Cause the alarm had gone off," the other agent had asked.

When Agent Valoze told him none of the team had come in, his trainee went to watch the security video. What he found was that one of the local police officers, who had been working as an undercover during the operation, had come into the warehouse in the middle of the night. He had free access to the warehouse, but his actions were still unusual. Not least of all when he grabbed two or three flat-screen televisions and took them out of the store when he left.

When the trainee reported these strange actions to him and showed Valoze the security footage, Agent Valoze said he would handle it and called the officer in to speak with him. This cop had been an asset to the investigation and worked as a task force officer with ATF for ten years, so Valoze knew there had to be a good explanation for what had happened.

"They're for the chief," the officer told Valoze and his partner Ralf, when he showed him the security video. "He wanted some TVs to put up on the walls at the station." And the bottom line was that all the swag used in the operation, including the refurbished televisions, technically belonged to the police department anyways. That's how Tom Lesnak had helped to set it up. Valoze and his partner worked with this officer for ten years, and they took him at his word. This officer had never been in any trouble and was absolutely beloved by the entire ATF Atlanta Field Division.

The trainee was not quite convinced of the officer's innocence and told Valoze that he was going to keep the DVD of the officer removing the televisions from the warehouse. Valoze told him that it was fine. Valoze was not the trainee's supervisor, and the trainee was free to report the incident to the resident agent in charge if he wanted to.

It wasn't like the TVs cost anything, and they were being used by an agency (the Savannah Police Department) who had invested man hours and resources into the case.

Valoze, who had other things to worry about at the time, had done his due diligence. He and Ralf questioned the officer about the incident and received an explanation that was satisfactory to them. The trainee, however, wasn't satisfied. Valoze recalls him as being very strait-laced, and completely by the book. So, he decided to keep a copy of the security footage.

Fast forward to the time when Ray and Valoze are interacting with the Italian mob in Cleveland. Meanwhile, down in Georgia, "the chief of police is getting jammed up in some gambling operation," Valoze says. "And the local cop [who had been working with them] got convicted for time fraud."

Apparently, the officer assigned to work with Operation Crossbones had been claiming all kinds of extra working hours, ripping off his own department and the ATF's federal funding sources. But he wasn't going to take these accusations lying down. In retaliation, "He dimed everyone out," Valoze remembers. "He brought up the affair, buying cars, and all sorts of baseless accusations."

If this guy's career was going down in flames, he intended to take as many other people as he could down with him.

Valoze explained the trouble to Ray and told him they would probably not be returning to Cleveland to finish the operation. Though he kept it to himself, Valoze knew the situation back home was about to implode because of his affair with the female attorney who had prosecuted both Operation Ceasefire and Crossbones. Remember, this was the same prosecutor who questioned him on the stand during one of the very rare trials that came out of those operations. It was also the same prosecutor who helped him apply for Ray Khan's green card the year before. In the end, things would end up getting much more serious than either Ray or Valoze had ever imagined.

CHAPTER EIGHT

Over the years, Ray has opened many doors for federal agents in complicated and in-depth undercover operations. Because of the opportunities he presented and due to his unique abilities, Ray was treated much differently than the usual informant. Ray developed a relationship with the people he worked with, which was based on trust. As a result of political unease and inter-agency accusations following Operation Crossbones, however, the agents' behavior towards Ray, and Ray's actions on behalf of the case, would all come into question. Agent Valoze's integrity was being directly challenged, and, as a result, everything Valoze had touched was fair game.

During Operation Crossbones, the agents had known that they needed to get Ray out on the streets where he could interact with potential targets, because, for these types of operations, that was an arena the agents couldn't enter themselves. To do this successfully, he was going to need some help to make a living. This is where Tom Lesnak's contributions came into the equation. He provided Ray with a van and sent him a steady supply of taxed and untaxed cigarettes he used for legitimate business and to draw out the criminal element the ATF were after. Ultimately, this would come under intense scrutiny years later when it was examined by the Office of Inspector General (OIG) and the Federal Bureau of Investigation.

These two federal agencies would waste nearly three years of manpower and millions of taxpayer dollars trying to find some impropriety committed by the agents in their dealings with Ray. They spent more money, time, and effort on this fishing expedition than the agents had spent on the undercover operation, and Operation Crossbones resulted in the seizure of hundreds of crime guns, as well as the removal of massive amounts of dangerous drugs and violent offenders from America's streets. And when it was all said and done, the OIG and the FBI would come up with absolutely nothing.

What is even more important to recognize is that Ray contacted these agencies himself and offered his statement voluntarily. As you read everything that follows and which details everything that these agencies put Ray through, consider the fact that, as a civilian, Ray could not be directly compelled to an interview. He could have easily lawyered up and not been approached or questioned by OIG or the FBI in this matter. Out of the goodness of his own heart, however, and in an effort to support Agent Valoze in the same way as he had supported Ray over the years, Ray Kahn contacted the investigating agents and offered to sit down with them. What followed would be extremely stressful for most people. But don't forget, we're talking about Ray Khan.

The HSI agent who worked with Valoze and Ray during both Operation Ceasefire and Operation Crossbones did the right thing to help Valoze and his undercover team: He contacted Ray and told him what was happening with Valoze.

Ray was mostly in the dark at this time. All he knew was that all of Valoze's operations had stopped suddenly. After Crossbones and their brief trip to Cleveland, Ray and his handler had been separated. As Valoze faced the accusations piling up against him, he withdrew from everyone around him. He lost forty pounds in a matter of weeks. He couldn't eat. He had given up trying to sleep. His personal life was in shambles, and it was becoming increasingly evident that his law-enforcement career might quickly be coming to an end. Despite being one of ATF's top producers for several decades, he was caught up in a tornado of politics, inter-agency bickering, overzealous investigators, and mounting accusations. It was a dark time, he will tell you, and one he tries to forget. What he doesn't overlook, however, are the people who stood by him. Among which was Ray Khan.

Unaware of the details of Valoze's investigation at this time, Ray began focusing on his slot-machine business. He wasn't privy to the insider network of the federal agencies, so he had no idea about the severity of Valoze's situation.

"All suddenly, all this problem happened," Ray remembers. "At that time, I had started a new business, so I'm working in my new business. And checking the news."

Every day, it seemed, there was a little more sensationalism about Valoze's case on the internet.

"Feds ID more than 200 cases in which prosecutor collaborated with agent with whom she had affair," The Florida

Times-Union published on February 15, 2015. [3] "US Attorney, ATF agent affair subject of investigation by Justice Department's Office of Inspector General" a WTOC headline from March 3, 2015, declares.[4]

This was all the public knew about the investigation, and Ray didn't know much more. He certainly didn't feel he could bother Valoze at that time, despite the years they had worked together.

"Because nobody talk to me about anything, so I don't know anything," Rays says. "Everyone just disappeared."

That was until the HSI agent called him and asked him to contact the FBI. The agent asked Ray to call the investigating OIG and FBI agents and to tell them everything that had happened during the two operations. Only then did Ray come to understand that his part in the undercover cases was being used against Valoze.

Ray was horrified. He had no idea he was being used as a tool in this witch hunt, and he was not going to sit back and let his handler, his friend, deal with this crisis alone. Ray told the HSI agent he would go to the FBI office to make a voluntary statement.

"I think they are giving to the Lou Sir hard time and all," Ray says, "and they try to tell me bad stuff about Lou Sir. But I really didn't know anything at all. That's not my business. My

---

[3] Jan Skutch. "Feds ID more than 200 cases in which prosecutor collaborated with agent with whom she had affair." *The Florida Times-Union*. March 3, 2015. Accessed August 10, 2025. https://www.jacksonville.com/story/news/2015/02/16/feds-id-more-200-cases-which-prosecutor-collaborated-agent-whom-she/15651143007/

[4] WTOC. "US Attorney, ATF agent affair subject of investigation by Justice Department's Office of Inspector General." *WTOC 11 The Southeast News Leader*. March 3, 2015. Accessed August 10, 2025. https://www.wtoc.com/story/28253788/us-attorney-atf-agent-affair-subject-of-investigation-by-justice-departments-office-of-inspector-general/

business is get the guns and drugs and all that. If I need anything, I ask Lou Sir for that."

Ray gave statements, repeatedly, but his involvement really had been that simple. He had no knowledge of the paperwork, the evidence collection, or the allocation of investigative assets. Ray's job was to bring people in.

Agent Valoze, however, knows exactly why the FBI and OIG investigators kept pushing Ray. "I guarantee you," he says, "if he had made something up about me, they would have given him his immigration status. That's a stand-up fucking CI right there." Valoze once again shakes his head as he recalls this time—a difficult time for him professionally and personally, to be sure. Yet his unassuming CI stood by him, just as he always had.

During this massive witch hunt, every email generated by the agents which pertained to Ray would be dissected and examined. For example, Ray participated in an undercover cigarette-trafficking investigation in Las Vegas for ATF Agent Tom Lesnak, who was, at that time, working out of the Virginia office. Tom was running an enormous undercover warehouse operation, Big South, out of Bristol and was responsible for backstopping and supplying merchandise for multiple other undercover ATF operations around the country.

Shortly after the Vegas operation, Tom sent an email to the Savannah ATF agents, stating, "I'm coming to Savannah, what can I bring Ray for a gift?"

It was an innocuous request. Ray had been moved all over the country at this point. While Vegas was certainly not Ray's least favorite assignment (he loves the glitz, the flash, and the society), Tom appreciated his help. The Vegas aspect of his case had arisen quickly, and Tom had no resources in the city at that time. He needed a reliable CI at short notice, and Ray, of course, had agreed to help. And, of course, Ray had delivered.

In response to Lesnak's email, Agent Valoze replied, "If you have an inexpensive laptop that he can use to set up an undercover email account, bring one." Lesnak had hundreds, if not thousands of devices at his disposal. Just like the counterfeit clothing, the pirated DVDs, and the expired food items in his warehouse, the electronics held no monetary value. So, thinking nothing of it, Lesnak brought a laptop back to Savannah for Ray.

The OIG would make a huge deal out of this email exchange, alleging that Ray was improperly "receiving gifts" from ATF, even though none of the refurbished electronics Tom had at his warehouse were obtained with government money. These were seized items donated by a private company for law enforcement use. The OIG knew that no improprieties had been committed, but this unjustified inquisition was being pushed by several corrupt attorneys at the US Attorney's Office in the Southern District of Georgia. Instead of trying to find out what actually happened during these operations and simply asking Valoze, their goal was to disgrace Valoze and oust the female prosecutor from her hard-earned position. Although they had basked in the glory and accepted awards and accolades for these operations, at the first sign of trouble they were now trying to distance themselves by making accusations of criminal misconduct by the agent and the prosecutor.

It is not the job of the United States Attorney's Office to conduct investigations, but that is exactly what they were doing. Mostly, Valoze will tell you, it seemed their investigation started small and ballooned as people found a way to exercise their professional jealousy. And for the next few years, the corrupt prosecutors at the US Attorney's Office in Southern Georgia would be the driving force behind this massive witch hunt.

Next came questions about the black BMW sedan. During Operation Crossbones, Ray told Agent Valoze he wanted to buy a BMW sedan that he could drive and then pass on to his son one day. Ray knew one of Tom's informants in Bristol, "Chris," had a car dealer license and often purchased cars from auctions. He asked Valoze if Chris could find him one, and Valoze emailed Tom to ask Chris. Three or four weeks later, Chris found a used BMW at an auction in Miami. Tom emailed a photo of the car to Valoze and, liking what he saw, Ray paid $52,000 of his own money for the car. He also paid Chris to have a driver bring the car to Savannah. Not that it matters, but Ray ended up using the car during most of his interactions with the future defendants of the undercover operation and always drove it when he accompanied the suspects to the warehouse for undercover transactions with the agents. ATF had absolutely nothing to do with the purchase or maintenance of this vehicle. Indeed, Ray had used his own vehicle and his own gas to support their investigation.

It should also be remembered that these were seasoned undercover agents who were sending emails to each other on their official government emails. All these agents understood fully well that everything done on the Department of Justice server is forever preserved. If they thought anything they were doing was improper, these agents certainly would have used a different method of communication. They weren't dumb. And they weren't doing anything wrong.

Yet, during one of OIG's numerous interviews with Ray, they pounced on him about the BMW and the emails, telling him that things were not supposed to be done that way. Ray didn't know how to respond. He could only tell them everything he and the agents had ever done was in furtherance of getting guns and drugs off the streets, and they had never hidden anything. They even told Ray that Agent Valoze had emailed a photo of the BMW to the involved AUSA and told her, "That's Ray's new ride."

Ray simply shrugged his shoulders, saying, "I don't know about any emails," which was true. OIG still demanded that Ray provide them with the BMW's VIN number. This was just yet another road the government went down, wasting time and the taxpayer's money. Again, this avenue of inquiry resulted in the obvious fact: There had been no wrongdoing on Ray's or the agents' part.

"They try to asking me the stuff," Ray remembers about the interviews. "Everything, too, I told them: 'Lou Sir is working every day, working hard and all this stuff, and there is nothing like you thinking someone steal money or anything. There is nothing.' We just use those cigarettes and everything to catch the bad guys or sometimes. We use the money to get the guns and drugs."

Even after several exhaustive interviews, one of the agents called Ray back and asked him again if ATF had helped him purchase the BMW.

"I told them again," Ray says. "You guys are totally misunderstanding it all."

It was more than clear that the OIG was not interested in Ray. They just wanted him to say something bad about Lou. Ray still went to each interview with a lawyer, though.

"Lot of stuff they are misunderstanding," he says. "So, I told them about that stuff."

Indeed, the investigating agents used Ray's cooperation to ask him about everything they could think of regarding the warehouses, including the merchandise they used to stock the shelves. "Where did that come from?" was their repeated question.

"They give it to us free," Ray says he told the agents. "And we used to give it free to people to come over there and talk about guns and drugs and all that. And I always load it up and go to the Savannah's bad areas and, if I see any kind of bad people, I hand it over to them free. Then I go like, 'Take a couple of shoes, man, and if you want more, come my warehouse.' And I have card, like a visiting card, like, come this address."

Inevitably, there came the questions about Ray's cigarettes and where they had come from. "Tom Sir sent that to us," he told the agents.

There was a little cultural disconnect here for the investigating agents as they interrogated Ray. The FBI would pay their informants, and they paid them well; but that didn't happen for ATF informants, and it didn't happen with Ray Khan. For this reason, the ATF had allowed Ray to sell merchandise (cigarettes) to help him make a living while he assisted in their cases. Indeed, the ATF maximum payment for any informant was $3,000 a month. It was infeasible for any CI to be able to work for many hours a month, without making a living at the same time.

"They would calculate living costs for their CIs," Valoze says. "In reality, they would be fucking those guys who couldn't keep the lights on."

When the opportunity arose, it wasn't uncommon for agents to help those good CIs to make a living.

In fact, the ATF didn't pay Ray at all, so the agents involved in the operations, with the full support of their chain of command, did what they could to help him make a living. After all, the method in which they helped Ray make some cash conveniently also helped him network to bring in people the operations were targeting.

But that wasn't the end of it. During yet another interview with Ray, the OIG agents brought up an email between retired ATF agent Bart McEntire and Agent Valoze. This email involved a $3,500 payment McEntire made to Ray for the job Ray had done for him in Los Angeles—this was the case involving the Chinese smugglers dealing in counterfeit Marlboro cigarettes. Bart was a former ATF supervisor who worked for Altria, which is the enforcement branch of Phillip Morris responsible for investigating counterfeit cigarettes. They routinely use paid "sources" and often work in conjunction with law enforcement throughout the world. So, just after Operation Crossbones, Bart reached out to Agent Valoze to ask if he could use the great Ray Khan for his investigation in Los Angeles. Bart stated he would pay Ray for his services and his expenses, the same as he pays all of his sources. As a result, Bart paid Ray $3,500—a fraction of what his cooperation saved his corporate employers.

The OIG and FBI started questioning Ray about this incident as if he had done something wrong. Ray explained to the agents he had flown to LA and met with Bart's "agency guys" and then contacted the "bad guys." The next day, he met with the Chinese nationals and was provided with samples of the counterfeit Marlboros. At Bart's direction, Ray would later buy twenty master cases of counterfeit Marlboros from the Chinese smugglers. Bart was pleased with the results and used Ray's information to continue his investigation. He paid Ray, who then returned home a little richer.

During the interviews, however, the agents continued to hammer on Ray, asking him why ATF didn't do anything with this case. They also asked him why ATF agents hadn't provided cover for him during this deal. Ray told them that ATF was not involved in this operation, and Bart's guys had covered him during the deal. When the OIG investigators asked Ray if he had been afraid of being "ripped off" during the deal, Ray laughed at the question. He told them this was just a counterfeit cigarette deal, and he had taken part in major gun and drug deals with real bad guys while working with Agent Valoze and the undercover team.

In fact, Valoze had no knowledge of Ray's LA trip until years later. Whereas it is typical for the FBI to use a single handler for an informant, the ATF, being a much smaller agency, couldn't operate this way—especially when they found a productive informant. They would pass Ray around to other agents for whatever they needed.

"It was a trusted network of ATF agents who shared informants," Lesnak says. "There was no need for everyone to know all parts of the operation. They were all responsible for their small parts of large operations. When they handed them [the informants] over, they didn't know what happened unless the agent decided to share the results."

Despite this fact, the investigators continued to bombard Ray with questions, just looking for anything they could use to fabricate some impropriety. They asked him if Bart helped him to buy the Marlboros he was selling in Georgia. Once again, they were fishing for something. Anything. Ray again told them that he bought his cigarettes through Big South, Tom Lesnak's company, as a part of his contract with ATF. He explained to them, once again, that selling cigarettes was one part of his mission. It allowed him to get the product out there in front of some of the "bad guys" and it also allowed him to make a living. This was getting more than repetitive.

And still the agents continued to press, asking Ray if he ordered cigarettes directly from Bart McEntire. Ray repeated he had signed up to sell product only for Big South. The OIG agent responded that Big South was just the "ATF Store." By this point in their inquiry, these agents knew damn well that Ray had no knowledge of the inner workings of Tom Lesnak's incredibly complicated operation, nor would he have any insight into how it was organized. They were just trying to get him to make some statement that would incriminate Valoze, Lesnak, or the other agents.

Another exhaustive line of questioning during these interviews revolved around, if you can believe it, the stale honey buns Agent Lesnak sent to Valoze for the new operation when it moved to the Port of Savannah. As ridiculous as it sounds, and it really does sound ridiculous, the OIG and FBI case agents became obsessed with these damn honey buns.

For background purposes, Lesnak would obtain palettes of honey buns, potato chips, energy drinks, and the like from companies which donated these items to be used in investigations across the country. All the items were near or past their expiration date, which meant they couldn't be sold. But they served their purpose for Tom and in other warehouse operations. If you were purporting yourself as a big import-export company, these cases of merchandise looked great on the warehouse floor. For this reason, Tom started shipping some of them to Operation Crossbones to bulk up the warehouse and its fake business. Again, while we are working within the framework of repetition which this inquiry created: These items had been donated and had no monetary value. The agents would simply move them around the warehouse to look like they had just arrived or were about to be shipped out. These items were stage props, a facade to make the import-export business look real to the targets.

When the items had been around for a certain period of time, or when rodents had started to get into them, the agents would remove them from the warehouse and place them in a nearby dumpster. Occasionally, Ray would ask the agents if he could have some of the expired honey buns. This meant there were fewer honey buns they would have to dispose of, so the agents gladly let Ray put some cases in his trunk. None of them ever asked or cared about what Ray Khan was doing with expired honey buns that the government had not paid for. But the OIG went after it like it was the case of the century. Ray tried to explain to them that these were perishable items which were expired and had no monetary value, but the interrogation continued until the agents realized they weren't going to be able to compel Ray into saying anything that would incriminate the agents.

"It wasn't Ray's job to know what happened with all the merchandise," Lesnak says. "You use CIs for their expertise. It wasn't his job to know what happened with the items. Even Lou didn't know what happened sometimes. I would be the one coordinating with the federal and state agencies across the country." But it didn't stop the FBI and OIG investigators from repeatedly peppering Ray with questions he could never know the answer to.

On numerous occasions, these investigators tried to convince Ray the ATF agents were not on his side and would claim they did not have his back. After working with Lesnak for a while, Tom told Ray he had been a special agent with the State Department before becoming an ATF agent. Later in the operation, Ray asked Agent Valoze if Tom could help him get a visa. Agent Valoze emailed Tom and asked him. The OIG agents showed Ray the response Tom had given, which said, "Tell Ray to hire a good attorney, it's been a long time since I've worked for the state department." It was an honest response, but the investigators tried to use it to turn Ray against the ATF agents.

As everything else they tried seemed to fail, the investigators really turned up the heat. When repetition, bullying, and coercion proved fruitless, they offered Ray what he wanted more than anything: status in this country. And all he had to do was to turn on the ATF personnel he had been working with. The FBI even talked to Ray's lawyer and told him they could help with his paperwork. Once again, Ray was told an agent of the government would take care of him. But, just like everyone else, they had underestimated Ray and his appreciation for all "Lou Sir" had done to help him over the years. Despite the fact the US Attorney's Office withdrew their support for Ray's S-visa application and he was, once again, facing deportation, Ray Khan stood tall for Agent Valoze and for ATF's operations.

"Truth is truth," Ray says. "They just didn't want to hear it."

"They wanted to be able to write up any violations that were committed," Valoze says.

"They wanted to leverage Ray's cooperation," Lesnak adds when the three men discuss this difficult time. "They offered him DOJ cooperation to get a green card."

"They were focused on not having proper paperwork," Ray surmises, "not on the actual results of the operation."

In truth, documentation of the non-monetary assets had always been a tricky part of the warehouse operations, and the movement of stock items between them was difficult to track, but none of the agents were educated in such management techniques. They were law-enforcement professionals, trained to purchase drugs and get guns off the street. They had never received classes on stock management or any of the business aspects of the operations.

"I would have welcomed an inventory specialist to assist with the operation," Valoze laughs, "but they didn't offer one."

As the men reminisce, they also remember some of the funny times.

"The cigarettes would get little bugs in them," Tom Lesnak recalls. "The tobacco beetle would lay eggs in them. When they would smoke them, they would pop."

"It almost added to your credibility," Valoze adds. "You'd sell cigarettes with bugs in them."

Lesnak laughs and agrees. "The government would never do this. That's how we would establish credibility."

The tone turns serious again as Valoze's mind goes back to the investigation. "No law-enforcement agency has ever put as much energy into a murder investigation that the OIG put into investigating me," he says. And Ray agrees.

What these investigators didn't know when they interrogated him, however, was that Ray Khan was not only loyal, but he was also not easily fooled.

CHAPTER NINE

It should come as little surprise at this point, but Agent Valoze remembers that, while the investigation into his professional conduct dragged on, Ray stood by his side.

"At my lowest point, Ray ended up counseling me," he says.

While Ray had considered "Lou Sir" a friend, Agent Valoze had done his best to maintain some level of professionalism and distance. He was an informant, after all, and Valoze had no illusions about Ray's continued quest to cut corners and make a few extra bucks here and there. By the time this investigation started, however, he thought of Valoze as family.

When asked when Ray believes that friendship started, Ray answers, "Right away. Right from Brunswick."

But when he was in trouble, Valoze kept his distance. He says now this was a matter of propriety, but he was also out of contact with everyone. As he tried to rebuild his life, he started small: with his family. Yet, the accusations dragged on, and Valoze's hopes for his career slid away.

"No cases, no problems. Big cases, big problems," says Lesnak as the men reflect on this time.

His words reveal a common ATF belief. There are agents who glide through their careers mostly unnoticed. You can stay in the middle of the pack, bringing in a few bad guys here and there just to keep your bosses happy. Or you can excel. This is the philosophy Valoze and Lesnak held. Unfortunately, these big cases also brought scrutiny, and that's what Valoze was facing as a microscope was placed over what seemed like every action he had taken since the days of Operation Statesboro Blues.

In January 2015, the AUSA with whom Valoze had an affair was suspended from her office and duties, initiating a whole new wave of investigations. Her government emails and phone were scoured, as were any testimonies she elicited from Agent Valoze during federal trials, the circumstances surrounding the dismissal of Ray's charges in 2009, ATF/AUSA involvement in staying Ray's deportation, and the subsequent S-visa application and paperwork. The AUSA herself was accused of falsifying an S-Visa application for an informant.

Valoze, the AUSA, and their chain of command had renewed Ray's paperwork with ICE every month since he had been released into ATF's custody. There had never been an issue or a question about the contents of this paperwork. Now, however, claims were made that important facts had been omitted purposely by the AUSA. In their accusation against this AUSA, the US Attorney's Office went so far as to claim she made false statements on these applications by omitting details of Ray's criminal history. This, they claimed, consisted of convictions for a crime involving moral turpitude, which would make him ineligible for an S-Visa.

In his response to these claims, the AUSA's defense attorney conducted an exhaustive analysis of Ray's history and the admissions and inclusions which were part of his monthly ICE paperwork. Much of this revolved around the AUSA's assertion that gambling is not a crime involving moral turpitude. Indeed, the attorney argued, gambling charges would be classified as regulatory and, as such, involved none of the evil intent or base, vile, or depraved elements which characterized crimes of moral turpitude.[5]

The defense team even consulted an immigration judge who reviewed Ray's monthly applications and supported the defense's claims. Eventually, the review committee agreed that Ray's papers had not been falsified nor were his historical crimes a basis for refusal of the applications to remain.

"I would do his paperwork every month," Valoze says, "to keep him legal here, and obviously now they wouldn't let me do it. ATF immediately canceled Ray as an informant, as soon as that shit happened. There's no loyalty at all, so they shut him down as an informant, they canceled their support for the S-visa, which wasn't happening anyway, but ironically, the two allegations against me both involved Ray."

In short, the allegations stated the AUSA lied by omission on Ray's S-visa application. This was clearly refuted by the immigration judge's review of the paperwork. The second allegation claimed the AUSA failed to elicit a complete testimony, thereby somehow committing perjury, during one incident when she

---

5 Such crimes which deny admission based on concerns of moral turpitude, at the time of this allegation, can be found in resources such as: Immigrant Legal Resource Center. "§ N.7 Crimes Involving Moral Turpitude." *Ilrc.com*. January, 2013. Accessed August 10, 2025. www.ilrc.org/sites/default/files/resources/n.7-crimes_involving_moral_turpitude.pdf

questioned Agent Valoze on the stand. Cast your mind back to the following exchange, which happened in a courtroom testimony for a defendant who was arrested during Operation Crossbones:

AUSA: What was the reason this informant [Ray] was working as an informant? What benefit would he receive?

Valoze: He received status in this country. To be here legally is the benefit.

The legal argument surrounding this apparently innocuous exchange was extensive. Specifically, the claim was made that the AUSA asked two questions and Valoze had only answered one: the second, which asked about the benefit Ray would receive. In their accusations, the US Attorney's Office claimed that the AUSA committed perjury by not requesting details of benefits Ray had received in the past through cooperating with ATF investigations. Yes, these accusations were that petty. And this AUSA remained suspended from a career she worked towards all her life due to arguments based on petty semantics.

But where did this leave Ray?

As the accusations and interviews revolving around the conduct of Agent Valoze and the AUSA continued, dragging through 2015 and into 2016, Ray needed to find work—and another way to remain in the country. His livelihood depended on it.

"In order to have license, my lottery license," Ray says, "I have to have work visa and all that stuff. Otherwise, they will cancel my license."

"Ray was kind of left hanging in the wind," Valoze agrees. "He needed someone to sponsor him and work with him."

In a turn of true irony, in 2016, Ray began working with Homeland Security Investigations (HSI)—the governing body for ICE. Yet Ray holds no resentment against ICE or the immigration process. In typical Ray style, he recognized only that he needed to obtain a work permit—and the sponsorship needed to keep the gambling license for his slot machines.

At this point, Ray's slot-machine business is just starting to bloom. His machines were slowly making their way into the convenience stores and gas stations of his network contacts but, being the ambitious Ray Khan we know, he was continuously trying to get more locations. At this time, however, he was still storing the machines in his garage and loading them into a trailer he towed behind his Cadillac. It was not the business of his dreams yet, and it would never become the empire he envisioned if he couldn't stay in the country.

Leveraging the contacts he had made while working with Valoze, Ray contacted Lesnak, who called a Homeland Security Investigations agent he knew in New Orleans. Lesnak only spent a little time telling "Scott" about Ray's potential, and Ray's previous results were more than enough to support his worth.

"These guys needed to work," Lesnak says, and it's unclear whether he's referring to informants like Ray, or HSI agents.

"I pay attention to my business after that," Ray says. "ICE don't do so much work."

Regardless, Scott agreed to take Ray on, and Ray started working for the very agency which constantly threatened his deportation. As soon as they realized his worth, Ray Khan became an official HSI informant, obtaining the sponsorship he needed by bringing them large-scale cases, the likes of which they had rarely seen.

"After a year or two," Ray says, shaking his head, "Scott was in Miami and got into accident. Big wreck. He was maybe forty."

Ray's first handler sadly died as a result of this crash. This time, however, Ray was transferred quickly, and Scott's trainee took Ray on.

It was easy work compared to what Ray had been doing with ATF. HSI didn't give him much to do physically each day. There was no moving pallets around a warehouse, and little face-to-face interaction with his new handler.

"I just talk to them by phone," Ray says. "And I have to go to Louisiana sometimes."

Between 2017 and 2018, Ray introduced HSI into a massive counterfeit-cigarette operation, in which contraband tobacco was being smuggled by the container load from Dubai into the United States. In 2018, Ray brought his HSI handlers an enormous money-laundering case with ties to London and Dubai. The suspects in these cases were Indian nationals Ray caught wind of through his typical convenience-store connections. How this man gained the information he shared with federal agents is amazing, yet it remains a mystery.

Despite all of this, however, he was still operating under the constant threat of deportation proceedings. He needed to keep producing so HSI would continue sponsoring his applications to remain in the US. To anyone else this would have been stressful. It may even have bred resentment against the US government, perhaps the country and the people. But this was just another day in the unusual life of Ray Khan. And things were about to get even more interesting.

Eventually, even the US Attorney's Office needed to admit the allegations against both Agent Valoze and the AUSA were going nowhere, and both were finally cleared of all accusations. Despite his exoneration, in 2017 Special Agent Lou Valoze elected to leave the position he held for more than a quarter of a century. Valoze officially retired from ATF later that year. He thought his interactions with Ray Khan were now in the past. However, the trouble surrounding Ray continued to affect Valoze's life, as well.

What was happening, you might ask, with the Department of Revenue? Where were they with their apparent persecution of Ray Khan? What was going on with the Georgia Good Ol' Boys? These are excellent questions. It will come as no surprise, but while Ray was excelling in his roles for the ATF and then for HSI, Billy Thompson's hard-on for Ray had become a severe case of blue balls. And he was leveraging all his influence to make trouble for our unlikely hero.

"I was big," Ray says, displaying his usual level of modesty. "That was why William Larson was targeting me, but now I learn that you don't need to be big or anything."

By this time, Ray had 225 different locations which were utilizing his slot machines. His business was going well. His work with HSI required little effort on his part and Ray was able to concentrate on growing his own company. Unfortunately, although he hadn't associated with Nital since his brother-in-law had (for all intents and purposes) stolen Ray's gas stations, bank savings, and Cadillac, Ray's familial relationship with Nital Patel was about to bite him in the ass again.

Beginning around 2014 (recordkeeping for this arrangement is extremely, and perhaps purposely, vague according to a 2017 law.com story titled "Macon Judge Declines to Disqualify Special ADA Over Legal Fees"),[6] William Larson, a private Atlanta attorney, had been contracted as a prosecutor by the Macon

[6] Law.com. "Macon Judge Declines to Disqualify Special ADA Over Legal Fees." *Yahoo! Finance*. November 17, 2017. Accessed August 10, 2025. https://finance.yahoo.com/news/macon-judge-declines-disqualify-special-074822449.html

County district attorney's office. You will remember Larson as the guy who kept returning to Ray's jail cell in Toombs County to demand a $300,000 fine. Around that time, Larson had also been looking into Nital. Over the years, his interest in Nital continued, and apparently, he kept digging until he once again came across a familiar name: Ray Khan.

"My brother-in-law," Ray says, "he did, like, a lot of wrong stuff." And due to the family connections and Ray's increasing business success, law-enforcement professionals in the Macon and Bibb County areas held fast to a belief that he was involved in Nital's shady practices.

In 2016, Billy Thompson received a promotion, moving up to the rank of special agent in charge of Georgia's Department of Revenue Alcohol and Tobacco division. Over the years, Thompson continued his friendship with Nital Patel. Indeed, their friendship grew to the point where the two were meeting socially most days and exchanging expensive gifts. Well... Thompson was receiving expensive items from Nital. But we are getting a little ahead of ourselves here. More on that juicy little nugget later.

For whatever reason, and apparently despite his professional successes, Thompson's obsession with Ray endured. Perhaps this was fueled by Thompson's continued association with Nital—that is what Ray will tell you. Over the years, however, his obsession continued to fester until, in 2019, Thompson tried to get to Ray through (now former) Agent Valoze.

Following his parting of ways with the ATF, Valoze invested much of his life savings into a new distillery business with an acquaintance who happened to be a lawyer. Having time to invest in the project, Valoze took on the role of distiller himself. Anyone in the hospitality business knows that the time leading up to the opening day for a restaurant, brewery, or distillery is fraught with financial peril. Over half of all these businesses fail in their first year. The startup costs are massive, and there is no guarantee of success, even if you should make it past those first twelve months. Valoze, as he does with any task, committed fully: financially, emotionally, and professionally.

"The owner [the lawyer] thinks it's cool: a retired ATF agent would be his distiller," Valoze remembers. "He sent me to South Carolina to learn," he continues, revealing he had no knowledge of distilling prior to that time.

While he was learning the technical aspects of the distillery, Valoze's new business partner used his legal knowledge to complete the required paperwork. "He did something, and we were fine with the feds," Valoze says, "but mistakes in the paperwork meant we weren't good in the state yet." But neither Valoze nor his partner knew about these mistakes. These paperwork errors. To anyone else, it might seem like a phone call could have solved the issue, but this wasn't enough for Thompson, who had a personal axe to grind.

Unaware of the DOR investigation going on behind the scenes, Valoze and his partner prepared for the opening day. Everything seemed to be going well, and they had planned a big event. Valoze's distilled products had been well received internally, and his stock of liquor, though still in its nascent stages, was hopefully sufficient to make it through the initial rush of interest they anticipated the event would produce. It had taken over a year, but they now had just days before their new venture opened its doors to the public.

Then Valoze heard fists banging on the doors.

"They were blocking traffic with their raid," Valoze recalls. "And these DOR agents had all their guns and tac gear and shit."

It was a full-blown raid on the new business. And it was headed by Thompson.

"DOR came in and made us pour out all the vodka we'd made," Valoze says. "It was Thompson."

"I'm just doing my job," Thompson had said as he watched Valoze empty the entire stock of the distillery down the drain. "It's not personal."

"Thompson's being real nice and all," Valoze cringes as he remembers the DOR Special Agent in Charge's face. "And I'm like, are you fucking kidding me?"

Of course, nothing came of the investigation, of the unnecessary raid. It was a paperwork error, after all.

"He was trying to say that Ray had some part of that business," Valoze says, though he hadn't seen Ray for over a year at this time.

"Thompson was obsessed with Ray at this point," Valoze says. He'd had nothing to do with Valoze's new, and now failed, venture. But then they really came after Ray.

Shortly after the raid on Valoze's distillery, Thompson's dream finally came true. All his efforts over the past seven years paid off when he contributed to the indictment of Ray Khan, and even Ray's son, on state RICO charges. He had been working behind the scenes with multiple local departments in Georgia to find allies in his mission to take Ray down. All the charges, unsurprisingly, involved allegations of gambling and racketeering. Thompson had become like the monomaniacal Captain Ahab whose obsession with Ray Khan had led him on an all-consuming quest to get his white whale.

In what started as a massive investigation initiated by Thompson, there were originally around one hundred store owners and other individuals also listed as defendants. The defendants were accused of not paying taxes on more than $39 million in profit, with this money allegedly coming from the profits of illegal video gambling machines in 2017–2018. During that time period, the Bibb County, GA, District Attorney's Office alleged customers spent more than $121 million while receiving $82 million in cash and prizes from these machines. It was alleged that the stakeholders and store owners for the companies and stores involved laundered the gambling profits, sending millions through trusts, and that no taxes were paid on this money.

"All to do with sales tax," Ray says, "but there is no product to apply the tax. There were a lot of other people with the 'master license' and no one pays sales tax. They didn't collect tax."

Aside from the tax-related allegations, Thompson's investigation also determined that the license holders set up "straw man" stores: locations which were established solely for illegally operating the gambling machines. The investigation claimed this allowed those accused to keep all the proceeds instead of sharing them with the store owners, which is required under Georgia law. This meant store owners missed out on their share of gambling proceeds. Additionally, it was alleged that the stores involved accepted funds from the license holders in exchange for putting the license holders' machines in their stores. The Department of Revenue claimed that money was not reported as income.

At the same time the Bibb County District Attorney's Office's investigation was ongoing. Thompson, who resided in Bulloch County, GA, was the driving force behind a separate-but-related investigation of Ray Khan and his associates in Bulloch County. Charges stemming from this investigation indicated that Ray Khan was involved in commercial gambling and operating a gambling facility. The allegations, which again involved illegal payouts, indicated the crime wasn't the possession of the video poker machines—that was just a violation of county ordinances governing businesses selling alcohol—but involved the manner in which Ray was giving payouts to the winning customers. Per Georgia state law, any payment in merchandise of more than five dollars in value is a felony offense. Additionally, the law states cash payouts in any amount are illegal.

According to documentation surrounding the investigation, Thompson and his crew had sent "confidential informants" to secretly videotape store personnel providing cash payouts to customers who won credits on the video poker machines. Supposedly, the county even sent warning letters to the store owners informing them that having the video poker machines on the premises was a violation of county law for stores selling alcohol.

After receiving this letter, Ray reportedly removed the machines from the convenience-store portion of the building, added to their number, and placed them in a gift shop next door. The gift shop was sparsely stocked with novelty items and clothing, such as T-shirts and caps. The confidential informants reported that, on one occasion, a young man was observed seated behind a counter while patrons walked past him into a back room. Inside the back room, there were signs displaying how many credits had been won from the video gaming machines and what any winnings could be exchanged for. A can of soda could be exchanged for two dollars' worth of credit; a small stuffed animal could be exchanged for ten dollars in credit from the machines. A jackpot of one hundred dollars' credit would get a winner a laptop computer, according to the sign. There was another sign which read: "No Cash Payouts."

According to the investigators, store customers would feed money into the video machine, choose the game, and touch the "play" button on the screen. Similar to any other slot machine, but without a handle, the screen displayed three sections where symbols spun around quickly, then stopped. If the three symbols matched, the player won that game. A player also had a choice to alter one section in an attempt to line up matching symbols. The gaming machines then offered players the option to use any credits they had won to play more games.

When the results of the investigation were made available to the public, a reporter from the Statesboro Herald contacted Ray by telephone. The reporter asked Ray about the allegations in the investigation, and Ray informed him that he did not own the gift shop where the machines were located. He further stated he had returned the machines that were inside his store to the company which owned them, telling the reporter, "We don't like to lose our beer license."

When the reporter asked Ray if he knew who owned the gift shop, he told them "some lady" who he did not know. Ray further stated that he never made much money from the machines. However, the investigators claimed Ray previously told law enforcement his wife owned the store. They said that, during an earlier inspection, Ray had stated he had opened the gift shop so his wife would have somewhere to work.

Something unexpected was about to happen, though. As the investigation gained traction, it became a force even Thompson couldn't control. And his shady practices were about to also come under scrutiny.

As different counties, agencies, and jurisdictions contributed to the massive investigation, it was revealed that there were corrupt law-enforcement officers and public officials entangled in this case. By the time all was said and done, Billy Thompson, a Bibb County deputy sheriff, a police chief, and the Bulloch County school safety director would also be implicated.

In the ultimate irony, Billy Thompson would find himself listed as a defendant in the same indictment as Ray Khan.

As the case entered the court process, a district attorney for the Macon Judicial Circuit revealed that during the investigation, it was discovered a Bibb County deputy was part of a bribery and tax evasion money-laundering scheme that "uncovered evidence of bribery and public corruption" in Middle Georgia.[7] The Bibb County Sheriff's Office stated that a deputy sheriff had been listed in a civil forfeiture action filed by the DA's office. Anthony Dalton, who was previously an officer with the Atlanta Police Department and had only minor infractions during his time there, was still in his probationary period with the Bibb County Sheriff's Office when he was announced as a defendant in the civil forfeiture action.

The Bibb County Sheriff's Office statement claimed they were aware that Dalton owned a convenience store but were not aware of his alleged involvement with any bribery and tax evasion money-laundering schemes. In the article, the sheriff stated, "Sometimes they just don't think or sometimes they may think that they're above the law." The above-mentioned civil forfeiture action included several other gambling master license holders as defendants. Together, they owned upwards of four hundred gambling machines in seventy businesses throughout Georgia. Dalton owned the RJS store at 2311 Pio Nono Avenue

---

[7] Helm, Claire and Jayla Whitfield. "DA: Bibb County deputy participated in bribery, tax evasion money laundering scheme." *WGXA News*. August 18, 2023. Accessed August 10, 2025. https://wgxa.tv/news/local/da-bibb-county-deputy-participated-in-bribery-tax-evasion-money-laundering-scheme

in Macon, one of three stores which were raided by investigators armed with search warrants.

Dalton would soon be arrested on racketeering charges pursuant to the same indictment which also listed Thompson and Ray Khan as defendants. The deputy's Bibb County Sheriff's Office hiring would come under scrutiny at that time because Sheriff David Davis agreed to hire him despite three Atlanta police supervisors saying he "shouldn't be in law enforcement."[8] Davis's response was that Atlanta police had not provided him with a complete file containing any details of their investigations before he hired Dalton.

Also charged in this indictment was then-Bulloch County Sheriff's Department captain Anthony Gray, who had since accepted a position as the head of school safety at Bulloch County Schools. The indictment stated that Nital Kumar Patel, Ray Khan's brother-in-law and arch enemy, had bribed Captain Gray in 2017. For this, Nital had received a Bulloch County sheriff's badge and deputy ID card, as well as help with traffic tickets and law enforcement protection.

Again, it cannot be overstated how ironic it is that Thompson was indicted on state RICO charges for racketeering. The man who had been so obsessed with Ray and who had tirelessly chased after him for all those years, Georgia Department of Revenue Special Agent in Charge William "Billy" Thompson, was charged with violating the state's RICO Act for Bribery in the same indictment. At the time of the final indictment,

---

8 O'Donnell, Bernie and Ensley Nichols. "Fired Bibb deputy's hiring under scrutiny after his racketeering arrest." *13WMAZ*. July 18, 2019. Accessed August 10, 2025. https://www.13wmaz.com/article/news/bibb-county-hired-deputy-despite-troubled-record-in-atlanta/93-2a700443-cb03-4568-a5d1-857f9246ff84

Thompson had been responsible for overseeing several southeastern regions of the Georgia Department of Revenue's Alcohol and Tobacco Division from January 2016 to July 2019. In the course of this extensive investigation which had initially been incited by Thompson's own obsession with Ray's gambling business, it had been discovered that the fifty-three-year-old special agent in charge exchanged "influence and information" with the one and only Nital Kumar Patel.[9] The indictment goes on to state that this favorable treatment had been given in exchange for multiple round-trip flights to Europe and a $13,000 Hublot watch.

According to Thompson's arrest warrant, Nital Patel used his influence to induce Thompson to investigate one of his main competitors, Ray Khan. It seems that bankrupting one of Ray's early business ventures and re-registering his Cadillac in his own name hadn't been enough for Nital. As Ray bounced back and his success grew, his rival's vendetta festered. Patel had provided Thompson with the airline tickets and the Hublot watch in exchange for Thompson's continued efforts to bring down Ray Khan. When Thompson lost control of the investigation, however, Nital's protection was also lost. In the end, both Nital Patel and Ray Khan were accused of participating in the same racketeering enterprise.

In its final version, the indictment alleged fifty-eight locations throughout the state of Georgia, including Bibb, Bulloch, Chatham, and Glynn counties, were a part of the racketeering effort. The district attorney stated that, for the state to provide coin-operated gambling machines, a license must be obtained.

---

[9] WTOC. "Ga. Department of Revenue agent arrested in illegal gambling investigation." *WTOC 11 The Southeast News Leader*. July 19, 2019. Accessed August 10, 2025. https://www.wtoc.com/2019/07/20/ga-department-revenue-agent-arrested-illegal-gambling-investigation/

Applicants must swear all the information on their applications is correct and that they are not delinquent in taxes. However, the indictment indicated that the defendants in this case—the store owners and their other locations—collected more than $3 million between January 2017 and March 2019, and that they had failed to pay taxes for that income. They were also accused of making false statements on their applications in 2018, 2019, and 2020 when they said they weren't delinquent in paying taxes.

The master license holders (of which Ray Khan was one) were also accused of making similar false reports, filing false tax returns and underreporting their income from the gambling locations. The charges against Ray and the others in the indictment also claim that master license holders paid the individual stores' license holders to keep the machines in the stores, which is prohibited by state law. Additionally, the indictment alleges the same master license holders owned some of the real estate where the machines were located and, in some cases, received rent payments from the location license holders.

In the end, the twenty-seven-count indictment, which was filed in Bibb County, Georgia, depicted an overwhelming picture of racketeering, false statements, money laundering, and illegal cash payouts which was alleged to be happening throughout Georgia. While it brought him a small measure of joy that Thompson and Nital were also indicted, Ray, it appeared, was not getting away from the charges Thompson's obsession had initiated this time.

CHAPTER TEN

Before the warrant for his arrest was issued, Ray started seeing people conducting surveillance on his house every time he or his family went outside.

"When I was there, they just keep following me," Rays says, his irritation mounting as he recalls the incident. "So, I just knocked on the car one time, 'Why are you following me?' They said nothing. I said, 'Why? Just tell me and I can tell my lawyer. Why you keep following me? If you need anything tell me.' They say no. I say, 'Why you standing outside of my house then? This is my property. Why you standing outside?' They say, "No, just checking." I say, 'What you checking? Tell me what you checking, what you need. I can give it to you.'"

Ray said no one told him why units were surveilling his house, and no one ever said why they sat outside his office.

"I told my lawyer, and he called William Larson," Ray said. "He threatened them with a lawsuit." Finally, Ray was able to afford good legal representation. His Atlanta law firm was expensive, but they were about to be worth every penny.

Ray was in the car with his personal assistant when he was notified that his house was being raided and there was a warrant for his arrest. The last time Ray had been arrested he'd spent months in an ICE facility. It had been lonely, uncomfortable, and he felt powerless. There was no way he could face that again. Instead of going home, he directed his assistant to head into South Carolina, and he started making phone calls.

"I know what they wants to do," Ray says. "They wants to arrest me and put me on an ICE hold."

He reached out to his attorney and to his controlling agent with HSI. Both of them advised Ray to lay low while they worked on getting things sorted out. That was all he needed to hear.

"They say, 'Bibb County people are very crooked,'" Ray says. "My lawyers say, 'They can do anything. So, you need to be careful.'" Ray shakes his head again as he recalls that day. "They can do anything."

Ray didn't even go home. He just told his assistant to start driving north. He didn't have a plan. He had nothing with him aside from his wallet, but he knew he wasn't going back to the ICE facility. He also knew the Georgia authorities would be coming after his assistant, having seen them outside his office on numerous occasions, so he directed her to drop him off at an exit in South Carolina. There he directed two other employees to pick him up. He also told them to bring him a large amount of cash. After a few hours, Ray's employees picked him up and drove him north to Virginia, dropping him off at the house of an Indian friend. There he devised his plan.

A few days later, armed with the basics of a scheme for his life as a fugitive, Ray took a train to New York City, arriving anonymously at busy Penn Station. He spent the last decade with undercover agents, and Ray had learned well.

"New York City is easy city to get lost," Ray says, when asked about this choice. He had a good friend in Idaho who also offered him a place to hide out, but Ray says this was his backup plan if the authorities ever located him in New York.

"Idaho is maybe thirty-six hours on the train," Ray says. Not his choice of ways to spend time. This is Ray Khan we are talking about, and by this time he was used to a certain standard of living. "Second plan. If something happened, I go to Idaho."

When he arrived in New York, Ray took his old cell phone to FedEx and mailed it to his son, Kamal, in Georgia. In the accompanying letter, he told Kamal to keep his phone activated. If it was tracked, he thought, law enforcement would think he was in his big house in Georgia. It was official. Ray was now on the run.

"It's easier to be a fugitive when you have a lot of money," Valoze says as he listens to Ray recount his time in New York.

Ray agrees. "Yeah, if you don't have money, it's always problem. If you have money, then like if you're smart and move properly and thinking it proper, then it's good."

And Ray Khan will tell you he used every trick he learned while working with ATF to help with his evasion tactics. The first thing he needed was a way to communicate with his lawyer and with his family, so Ray went to Jackson Heights and found a small electronics store where he purchased two burner phones. He used the first phone to create a WhatsApp account, using that phone's number for the account. Then, he set up WhatsApp on his second phone, again logging in with the phone number from the first phone. He kept the first phone only long enough to verify the number for WhatsApp, then took it apart and threw it into the nearest trash can. Now, even if someone intercepted his WhatsApp messages, Ray's location couldn't be tracked using the phone number associated with the account.

"He was becoming the Indian Jason Bourne up there," Valoze laughs.

Once Ray had his phone set up, he moved into a hotel on Columbus Circle.

"Very nice area," Ray assures, in case anyone was concerned that he might be slumming it. "Walking distance to everywhere."

He had no desire to drive and risk getting stopped by police, though sometimes he did take the subway using a monthly pass he purchased—no name necessary. When he saw police officers, Ray will tell you, he just turned around and walked the other way. For a few days, everything seemed to be going well. Then, law enforcement in Georgia tried to arrest Kamal.

"They just trying to get to me," Ray says.

Thinking they could draw Ray out by arresting his son, the local authorities, however, had failed to do their homework. They intended to jail Kamal as an illegal immigrant, believing Ray would come out of hiding to assist in his release. The flaw in this plan was that Kamal had been born in the United States.

"They brought ICE agents to the house," Ray says, "and they were like, 'No, this kid was born here.'"

When asked about his family, Ray admits his son, Kamal, is not tough like him. He didn't like the situation his father was in, was nervous when he nearly got arrested, and had a hard time dealing with the demands of keeping Ray's whereabouts a secret. But, being Ray Khan's son, he dealt with it. In contrast, Ray says his wife was not scared at all.

"My phone, I leave it in my house," Ray says. He had Kamal plug the phone in to keep it charged and then put it into a drawer where it simply remained. Eventually, the Georgia law-enforcement authorities, probably through the urging of William Larson, who was still acting for the District Attorney's

Office at this time, would think about tracking Ray's device in an attempt to locate him.

"They track my phone, and they see it and they think, 'Ray's house is so big, he must be somewhere hiding there in the house,'" Ray recalls.

Police officers with their K9 partners arrived at Ray's home, where his wife opened the door for them. Despite her assurances that Ray wasn't there, the officers conducted a thorough search, using their dogs to attempt to sniff Ray out.

"They are stupid," Ray laughs. "They are like two, three hours at my house." Of course, Ray was nowhere to be seen, and Larson was left frustrated once again.

Following this event, however, Ray doubled his efforts to keep his location a secret. When his lawyers said they needed Ray to sign papers, Ray would contact his wife.

"I always like tell my wife to go online buy the ticket for any kind of train," he says. "Any name. Get the ticket, train ticket, New York to Savannah. I never used my name anywhere."

Ray's wife easily went along with his plans. She even thought the subterfuge was fun.

"I come early morning here [to Georgia], five o'clock," Ray goes on, "and I have my guys who work for me. They knows I coming. So, they are over there all night checking out Amtrack station so no police, anything. And I go to Savannah."

Ray hopped the train in New York, with his ticket in whatever name his wife had devised in his hand. The conductors never checked for identification, as long as the ticket was valid. He'd arrive in Savannah and meet with his employees who would bring along whatever paperwork required his attention. When needed, they'd bring a notary with them. Then Ray would wait in their car until the train arrived to take him back to New York.

Only once he was safely back on the train would he send the paperwork back to the authorities.

"I take my train, the 9:30, and then I send it," Ray says, speaking of the paperwork. Once he was safely over the Georgia state line, the paperwork would be delivered by his employees. "And William Larson sees that and thinks the Ray is in Savannah," Ray laughs.

Ray says he did this five or six times over the four months he spent on the run. "They think Ray is in Jacksonville or South Carolina," he says. But Ray kept his true location a close secret. He never told his lawyers where he was. Only his wife and his driver knew.

Driver? You might ask. This is Ray Khan we are talking about. And when you tip as well as Ray does, people remember you.

Ray had cash with him, and he collected more from his employees each time he took the train to Savannah. If we know nothing else about the great Ray Khan, we know he loves both making and spending money.

Ray had been to New York City multiple times and, during those vacations with his wife and family, he hired a driver to show them around.

"Muslim," Ray recalls of the driver, "from a different country."

Having driven Ray around for a few days during his previous visits to New York, the driver knew him and was more than happy to help when Ray needed him. He was also aware how well Ray would compensate him for his time.

"I know that nobody knows about that driver," Rays says. "I already called him told him find nice apartment [a suite in a hotel] and lease it in your name." It was a bold plan, which relied on someone Ray did not know well. Ray makes friends quickly, though, through his odd mix of straight talk and charisma.

So, his driver acquired accommodations, and Ray's name never showed up anywhere. This was how Ray managed to stay under the radar. But what did he do all day?

"I have to kill the time, you know," he says. "If I by myself then I can walk around by myself, and I just make the friends in those restaurants. Because I don't want to make any kind of friend who keep asking me anything. So, I always just make the friends in the restaurants or bars, you know."

Ray's wife was staying intermittently in Maryland and taking brief trips back to Savannah, but she would also visit Ray in New York on the weekends. The rest of the time, Ray had people who would help him out.

"I do shopping every week, and my wife when she comes up, she brings me cash money [from his business]."

And Ray is living in style. "Every day go to the nice, nice bar, drink and talking to people," he says of his time in the Big Apple. "Make some friend at the bar. That's it. Managers and all are my friends. So, most of bar, Rockefeller Center, they have bar at the top, so I go there. They don't charge me anything. They give me all kind of good food, but no charge."

Ray paved his way through the city in large tips. In return, he found people who helped him everywhere. He treated them well when he was there before, and when Ray needed it, they returned the favor.

After a few weeks, Ray's driver located a furnished apartment in midtown Manhattan for Ray and continued to rent it in his name, keeping Ray invisible. Ray didn't really know anyone else in New York City. But along with his inner strength, Ray has always had that unique ability to make the best out of any situation.

It wasn't long before Ray developed a new daily routine in his Manhattan neighborhood. Each day, he spent his time visiting coffee shops, taking walks through Central Park, and eating at midtown restaurants. As always, he charmed people and made connections. He also continued to run his business in Georgia by phone. His loyal employees would sometimes make quick trips to New York to bring him more cash. Yet, although his living conditions were better than the average person, he was still a fugitive of the law.

Over the weeks, and then the months, Ray remained in touch with his high-powered attorneys in Atlanta. While he hid out in New York, his legal team were conducting their own investigation into the conduct of Billy Thompson and John Willis, the investigating agents of Georgia's Department of Revenue. They were also looking into some of the police officers in Georgia who had been involved in the case against Ray. Their findings would ultimately set Ray free and dismantle the entire investigation. But for now, Ray was hiding from the law a thousand miles away from his family. While his time as a fugitive in New York would be mostly uneventful, there was one very close call.

Back in Savannah, Ray's house was still under constant surveillance by the DOR agents. Now his office and his personal assistant's office were also being watched. The Georgia authorities knew Ray had skipped town, and they were desperate to find him. They were going through cell phone records and utilizing all the technology available to them to locate Ray through cell phones, banking and credit card activity monitoring, and even facial recognition software. To this day, Ray doesn't know how they figured out his location, but one day men with badges came looking for him at his building.

One afternoon Ray was taking his walk through Central Park when his phone rang. It was the daytime doorman at his building. Just as he was when visiting bars and restaurants, Ray was a generous tipper at his home base. He had gotten very close with all the doormen but developed an especially friendly connection with the one who was calling him. The doorman told him that two NYPD police officers had come to the building and shown him a photograph of a man who looked very much like Ray. The officers asked the doorman if this individual was a resident of the building. The doorman told the officers that he did not recognize the man in the picture as a resident, but that there were many middle eastern and Indian residents, and he couldn't be sure. He told the officers that the building manager would be on the premises the next morning and that they should return then to speak with him. He told Ray he provided the officers with the manager's card and the officers left.

Ray thanked the doorman and immediately called his loyal driver. Ray knew that the Georgia authorities had no jurisdiction in New York, and he guessed they had somehow located him and called the NYPD, but Ray did not panic. He instructed his driver to pick him up on the other side of Central Park and take him to a hotel. They went to several hotels before they were able to get a room, using the driver's credit card and identification, of course. Ray then instructed the driver to go to his apartment later that night and retrieve his cash, clothing, and jewelry. It had been a close call. Ray would remain in his new hotel for several weeks as he tried to figure out his next move.

Soon, however, he would receive some life-changing news from his attorneys in Atlanta that would make his decision an easy one. Ray was about to be a free man.

"Meanwhile, my lawyers are fighting very hard," Ray says. His well-paid legal team was firing at the indictment from multiple angles. Larson, who was acting as the prosecutor, and the judges were getting tired of it all. The prosecution was losing the legal arguments against Ray's Atlanta-based lawyers, which included issues with the jurisdiction of the charges as listed in the indictment. They were slowly wearing down the indictment and those involved in the hearings. Yet still, the prosecution kept adding more charges to Ray, trying to chip away at his resources and the defenses his lawyers presented.

Then, the Department of Revenue ordered a tax audit of Ray and his business. If they couldn't get Ray, they reasoned, they would at least get his money.

The audit was, as would be expected, grueling. The DOR auditors requested thousands of documents, taking up more and more of Ray's attorneys' time (and costing Ray more and more money). Now Ray was also paying accountants who specialized in this type of tax-based investigation and were working with his attorneys throughout the audit. Meanwhile, Larson and his investigators were still looking for him.

As was true in New York, Ray also had loyal people in Georgia. In attempts to mislead the investigators, Ray's acquaintances would fabricate stories about seeing him around town in different places. And they would ensure the information got to Nital, who was more than willing to pass it along.

Those guys still work for Ray. "They was like kind of making fun of them," Ray admits.

Eventually, after several weeks, the audit of Ray and his business was completed, only to find that Ray had overpaid his taxes. The DOR couldn't get Ray, and now they had failed to get his money, too. Indeed, all they had done was make themselves look foolish, and now they had to provide a tax refund. It was a joyous moment for Ray's legal team, though the almost $50,000 Ray was owed wouldn't even make a dent in the fees they were accruing.

Then Ray's attorneys found a crucial piece of information—one which would ironically get the charges against Thompson dropped, as well as those against Ray and the other indictees.

In the course of their investigations, Ray's lawyers investigated John Willis, the Department of Revenue's special investigations director. At this time, Willis was Thompson's boss and one of the law-enforcement officials who had leveled the charges on the indictment. While combing through his employment history, an investigator on Ray's legal team uncovered a surprising fact: Willis lied on his paperwork when he applied for a promotion to the director position within DOR. On that application, according to a press release from the OIG on March 15, 2020, Willis claimed to have a two-year criminal justice degree from the University of Northwest Florida. Willis, however, had no such qualification.

The OIG press release concludes, "Providing false information on an official state document is a crime and the matter has been forwarded to the Attorney General's Office for possible prosecution."[10]

Ray's attorney filed motions, and according to Ray, no one even spoke during the next court hearing. There were no questions, and no arguments. The judge walked into the courtroom and then dismissed everything. Ray's lawyers had gotten everyone's charges dropped. It cost Ray almost $3 million for

[10] Office of the Inspector General. "Revenue Investigations Director Terminated After OIG Investigation." *Georgia.gov*. March 15, 2020. Accessed August 10, 2025. https://oig.georgia.gov/press-releases/2020-03-15/revenue-investigations-director-terminated-after-oig-investigation

his lawyers to get him out of the indictment, but he reveals this figure with no regret.

But what about Thompson?

"One time Tom Sir [former ATF agent Tom Lesnak] give me four watches with the box and all," Ray says. "One time my brother-in-law came to my house, and I just give it to him. And after that, that watch goes to Thompson and he get caught with this watch." This was the watch mentioned in the bribery charges which were later leveled against Thompson.

"Thompson got tickets to Las Vegas," Ray adds, mentioning Nital had paid for these items. All of this had been revealed in Nital's statements when he got wrapped up into Ray's indictment. "Nital trying to make out that Thompson is his friend," Ray says.

When asked if he regrets Thompson's charges being dropped, Ray denies that it affected him at all. "Thompson is too small in front of me," Ray says now. "He cannot give me hard time."

In truth, Thompson got cuffed and perp-walked in front of cameras. He was charged with offenses relating to corruption and bribery. He would have been convicted and put in prison if his charges had been separated from Ray's. In a way, though, justice was served. Thompson got no pension. The Department of Revenue arrested him and fired him immediately. It was the same fate which had befallen John Willis. Both men had been with DOR for a long time, but both had ultimately felt the repercussions of their actions.

"When you make things personal like that—and it was obvious with Thompson it was personal with Ray," says Valoze, "when you do that, your shit better be really clean. You're opening yourself up. And Thompson, he opened himself up and he got burned."

CHAPTER ELEVEN

"We had a good run," says Tom Lesnak when he thinks back to the days of ATF's long-term warehouse investigations. "Thank to guys like Ray, we had a good run."

Valoze agrees. They really made some great cases, and much of their work was done on the backs of informants. Usually, however, those informants had specific qualities and targeted uses in the cases. Ray Khan was an exception.

"Ray could do the business part," Valoze says, "and he could do the stolen-guns-on-the-street part, too." He truly was an outstanding ATF informant.

So, what is Ray doing now?

He just can't help himself. Ray is still an unpaid, yet highly effective, federal informant. His former HSI handler, Scott's assistant who took over after his death, was promoted and moved to a new, highly coveted, position in southern Europe. But Ray has a new handler in the Louisiana office. And he's still bringing in massive cases.

"Dubai is the business hub right now," Rays says. And he should know. "Last twenty years, I am stuck here," he goes on. It was not until 2023 that Ray finally got his green card. "And when I got my papers, I went to India a couple time. Two times Dubai and once to Turkey. I always go to very nice bars there. Like Burj Khalifa, one hundred twenty-second floor. There is a very nice bar you can sit, and they give you all kind of food like different food, they keep giving it to you all the time."

It's classic Ray Khan.

When he's not exploring his newfound freedom around the world, Ray continues his work with his slot-machine company and helps Homeland Security Investigations on the side. The cigarette case from 2017, he recalls, was a long case. The smugglers were using shipping containers to import counterfeit cigarettes—Ray's specialty. Those involved in the scheme trusted Ray enough that they sent him samples, which he then sent to HSI. It took the investigations team two years to build the case, but the suspects were arrested and charged, thanks to Ray.

His most recent HSI case involved people from, of all places, Guyana. This investigation was based in Florida and involved someone who had approached Ray through his business.

"Because I have machines, the big business, so I travel a lot," Ray says. "I go everywhere. So those Guyana people met me few years ago. They met me and they offered me like millions of dollars. He say, 'You have got the big business, if you need the cash money.' They say, 'I am talking about five, ten million dollars, if you need it.'"

It makes sense. High-cash-flow businesses have always been targets for money launderers. These typically include car washes, laundromats, and, for some reason, nail salons. But nowhere is there a greater cash flow than in gambling. Casinos, of course, are constantly aware of people washing money through their locations. They have investigators and they train their employees to recognize the signs. How about unattended slot machines, though? There is no one present to monitor their use. And what about the businessmen behind this ready cash industry? It makes a logical kind of sense that Ray should be approached, but knowing Ray Khan, it was just a matter of time.

"They have the money," Ray says. "I have to wash it."

The plan in this case required Ray to open an HSI-monitored account with money given to him by the Guianan suspect.

"Once we do like two hundred thousand two or three times," Ray says he told his handler, "They will trust us. Then he give us like million, two million to do same thing. That was the plan."

Unsurprisingly, however, the federal government managed to get in its own way.

"And then, like, the Louisiana HSI people call me, and they say very big boss from Washington, DC, wants to talk to you, and I say, 'Who is this guy?' They say, 'It's very big guy. Let me connect the phone with him and you can talk to him.'"

Ray says he spoke with this high-ranking HSI agent working out of the capital. The agent asked him if he would be willing to work with the agents in Florida. Ray was amenable, but a little wary as he didn't know any of the Florida HSI team. He was used to dealing with his handler in Louisiana, and he felt he needed to get to know someone before he could introduce them as "his people" to a criminal. For that reason, Ray asked if the agents in Louisiana and those in Florida could work together. They refused.

"You cannot meet the Ray," he says his Louisiana contacts told their counterparts. For some reason, he says, his handlers didn't trust the agents in Florida to keep Ray safe during the deal.

Valoze suspects this was more of a professional jealousy issue, however. The Louisiana team stumbled upon an excellent informant, and, unlike ATF, they didn't play nicely with other agents working in different offices. This was incomprehensible to Ray, who had traveled the country to work with different ATF field offices.

In the end, Ray said the Guianan money launderer was arrested, but he insists it could have been a much bigger case.

"One guy [the Guianan] offered us like ten million dollars at one time. So, we make plans. 'Do we have plane?' I ask the Louisiana [HSI agents], and Louisiana say, 'Yeah, we have plane." So, I say, 'We can fly to Orlando Airport, small airport. Me and that guy come with the ten million dollar. We put it in the plane and we fly back to the Louisiana.' Simple, and we all going one plane. And Florida office is making all this problem."

Ray's faith in HSI seems to have diminished after this incident, as he knows most cases he brings them will cross jurisdictional lines. For example, in another case, Ray offered to help one of his "acquaintances" with laundering $10 million. On this occasion, Ray says HSI agents were listening to him talk to the suspect using a bug in Ray's car. As the conversation progressed, the agents recognized the name of the man Ray was talking to and realized it was someone they'd previously investigated. Unfortunately, the agents had been unable to find a way into the suspect's organization to build their case. Ray provided them with that access but, due to jurisdictional issues, the case fell apart.

"ATF is not like that," Ray remembers. "I say I'm coming tomorrow morning, they ready tomorrow morning."

"Feds are their own worst enemy," Valoze agrees, though he and Lesnak admit that wasn't the case with the ATF of their time.

It's a different time, even just these few years removed. "Each office is very territorial."

Ray says he has the next case lined up for HSI, once they are done with the prosecution of the Guianan.

"Jewish people," he says, with his usual tact. "They look very simple," he goes on to say. "They are from Pennsylvania—they have marijuana farms in California, armed security people. They have lots of cash they can't put into the bank."

While marijuana has become legal in many states across the US, it remains federally illegal and is classified as a Schedule I Controlled Substance by the DEA. For that reason, most federally insured banks will not permit company accounts with ties to the marijuana industry—and there is a lot of money in that industry. This requires the money to be laundered prior to being deposited into a bank. As long as the money is one step removed from the marijuana industry, the bankers are none the wiser.

"We already identify everything and I already give it to Louisiana [HSI agents],' Ray says of his new case, "but it's going to be same problem happen. Because Pennsylvania, if they go and try to do anything, or California. So, Louisiana say, 'We try to do something, and the same thing happen.' So why do anything?"

The frustration is clear, not just for Ray, but for the retired agents who are listening to his story.

"I keep the relationship still," Ray says of his Louisiana HSI connections. "If I use it, or not, but still keep it."

With regard to his immigration status, Ray now has what's called "special advanced parole." Once again, it is a status which needs to be renewed every year.

"He shouldn't have to do that," Valoze says. "You would think with all the cases Ray helped with—the guns, drugs, home-invasion crews, car-theft rings. You'd think there would come a point where the US government would say, 'We're going to help you.' That never fucking happened. Ray is only here because Ray succeeded and did this all on his own. I didn't help him," Valoze continues. "He's here because of him."

And it's true. Still now, the US government has done nothing to help Ray Khan with his immigration problems. Ray's application and status has only advanced because of the fact his entire family consists of US citizens. His wife and his children are all American, born and raised in the USA. Yet Ray still needs to apply every year to remain with them. The big red "DEPORTATION" stamp in his records, which could have been expunged by any AUSA he has worked with, still haunts him, flagging his application at every step of the interminable process.

"With Ray, the US government made commitments to protect him, and he did the things they asked, and they still fucked him," Valoze says. "A massive amount of time was simply spent trying to un-fuck it."

So, why does he do it? After all that has happened to him over the years, why does Ray Khan keep bringing bad guys to the table? Why does he risk his life, and the well-being of his family, for a government which has done nothing for him? Ray quickly worked off his petty counterfeit-cigarette charges, so why is he still doing it?

"Some of these guys genuinely believe in the work we are doing," Lesnak offers as an explanation. "They live in the same community as we do."

Indeed, Ray will admit he sometimes has safety concerns for himself and his family. He risks running into bad guys in his daily life, but he still lives in the Savannah area. And his drive to help the US government remains, somehow, intact.

"I think we abused Ray, and we abused his motivation to work," Valoze says, "and we abused the fact that his motivation to work went far beyond his charges."

The former agents agree on this. There was no need for Ray to keep coming back, to keep bringing them bigger and bigger criminals for their cases. But Ray was never a typical informant.

Informants are usually bad people who are guilty of some "violent shit," as Valoze says. "Then you get this guy who is very different. You can trust him. And when he had the chance to throw me under the bus and benefit from it, he stood up tall."

"I'm sitting here today," Lesnak says, "because there are guys who went over and above. Ray's gain in working with the government will never, ever meet the risk he put himself in."

And this strange relationship has stood the test of time. It somehow became a tale of friendship between a handler and informant.

"If an informant screwed me over," says Valoze, "in turn, I had no choice but to screw them over. I've also protected them when they do what they said they were going to do." And Ray was one of those informants. During everything they have been through together, Valoze always did what he could to help Ray, and his informant recognizes his efforts.

"No, but those people help me," Ray says, nodding towards Valoze and Lesnak as he speaks. "I have to remember that. So, if they need anything, if I could do anything. I could just do it. Now I have businesses, and these people trust me."

"Most people don't think like that," says Valoze. "That's very rare, right? He has every right to be bitter about the way this government has treated him. He's never received any accolades or that hero's return that he so deserves. But he is still sitting here, still willing to help law enforcement to make this country safer. If I re-entered the world of undercover law enforcement tomorrow, he would be right there at my side."

"This is what makes it fascinating," Lesnak agrees. "This relationship. It makes it different."

Ray and Valoze then share a laugh as they remember a time they went to Vegas together on an operation and got drunk afterwards. "We go to one of those oxygen bars to help our hangover," Ray remembers.

The ease Ray displays around Valoze is evident. The history the men share is apparent in the way they interact, even when speaking about the tough times they have endured. Their friendship shines through in the memories they share. Indeed, when asked whether Ray would change anything if he could go back and live his life again, he immediately shakes his head.

"I would never have met the Lou Sir," he says. "Never get the chance to work with that kind of people or anything."

"If we asked Ray to do it," Lesnak concurs, "my guess is he'd still do it today. But it's a one-way agreement."

And he's right. On one hand the informant might get to do things they would never be able to do in their daily life—all over the world.

"They get pulled into it and the adrenaline," Lesnak says. But he goes on to say that the confidential informant agreement is a one-sided contract. "It tells them all the things they cannot do. There's nothing in there about what they [the government] will do if they honor their agreement."

If ATF asked him to help, though, Rays says, "I can help. ATF helped me like ten, fifteen years. I can still help. I don't have any problem with that."

At his core, Ray is simply a good man. He came from a good family, and Ray thinks his police officer father is likely very proud of the work he has done with these federal agencies. But Ray also recognizes his life is unusual.

"Lot of ups and downs," he says, minimizing all that he went through. "If I try to tell someone, no one believes me. They say just I'm dreaming, or lying, or watching too much movies."

Once Ray's immigration status in the United States is finally secure, he says he is considering spending a lot more time back in India. He wants to return to his hometown in Gujarat, which he says looks like New York now. Everything is very cheap over there, Ray would tell you, and he would be a very rich man in Ahmedabad.

"In India I have cooks, drivers, massage therapists," he says. And Ray misses the Indian culture, too. "People are all sitting together at night, spending time together."

Ray wants to give his children experience with his Indian culture so they will pass it down to future generations. He almost has an ideological view of the country, however, like many foreigners living abroad. "No alcohol," he says of Gujarat, "and there are no drugs in India."

A simple internet search would show these statements are not truly rooted in fact, but this is Ray's viewpoint, and it's clear he regrets not having been able to visit Ahmedabad more often. "Not too much poverty in Gujarat," he says. "Poorer people had land, and they were able to sell it and make money. Land there is expensive now."

Meanwhile, Ray spends all day, every day, working to promote one of the "six or seven" companies he says he now owns. He's now leveraging his contacts for his own purposes and is putting slot machines in convenience stores and gas stations throughout Georgia. While the state lottery takes 16 percent, Ray and the store each get half of the remaining profit. It's a good business to be in, Ray will tell you, as he admires his custom-built Rolls Royce.

"That was exciting every day," he says. Thinking back on the days he spent working in the warehouse with Agent Valoze and his team of undercover operatives.

"The three of us could open up a warehouse right here and we would absolutely kill it," Valoze jokes. And with Ray by their side, it's undoubtedly true.

"I always tell the Lou Sir," Rays jokes, thinking back about how they met, "if you want me to work why did you arrest me? You should've just tell me that. Why don't you work with us? And we are good to go and we can do it together."

"It wasn't about you," Valoze says, "I just wanted your Cadillac."

"I just bought it like fifteen, twenty days ago," Ray laughs, thinking of his first Cadillac. "No mileage, nothing."

***

Ray's story is an unusual tale, to be sure, and it's one we don't usually get to hear. Indeed, as Lesnak will tell you, "The story has never been told from the informant point of view."

"Ray worked all of his charges off," says Valoze. "Probably in the first gun deal he ever did, and then he just kept on going."

This is the story of Ray Khan—possibly the greatest informant the government has ever had.

And he isn't finished yet.

BIBLIOGRAPHY

ALM Media. "Macon Judge Declines to Disqualify Special ADA Over Legal Fees." *Yahoo! Finance*. November 17, 2017. Accessed August 10, 2025. https://finance.yahoo.com/news/macon-judge-declines-disqualify-special-074822449.html

Bureau of Alcohol, Tobacco, Firearms and Explosives. "Contraband Cigarette Trafficking Act." *ATF Bureau of Alcohol, Tobacco, Firearms and Explosives*. Last updated September 28, 2022. https://www.atf.gov/alcohol-tobacco/contraband-cigarette-trafficking-act. Accessed August 10, 2025 Accessed August 10, 2025.

Helm, Claire and Jayla Whitfield. "DA: Bibb County deputy participated in bribery, tax evasion money laundering scheme." *WGXA News*. August 18, 2023. Accessed August 10, 2025. https://wgxa.tv/news/local/da-bibb-county-deputy-participated-in-bribery-tax-evasion-money-laundering-scheme

Immigrant Legal Resource Center. "§ N.7 Crimes Involving Moral Turpitude." *Ilrc.com*. January, 2013. Accessed August

10, 2025. https://www.ilrc.org/sites/default/files/resources/n.7-crimes_involving_moral_turpitude.pdf

Jan Skutch. "Feds ID more than 200 cases in which prosecutor collaborated with agent with whom she had affair." *The Florida Times-Union*. March 3, 2015. Accessed August 10, 2025. https://www.jacksonville.com/story/news/2015/02/16/feds-id-more-200-cases-which-prosecutor-collaborated-agent-whom-she/15651143007/

O'Donnell, Bernie and Ensley Nichols. "Fired Bibb deputy's hiring under scrutiny after his racketeering arrest." *13WMAZ*. July 18, 2019. Accessed August 10, 2025. https://www.13wmaz.com/article/news/bibb-county-hired-deputy-despite-troubled-record-in-atlanta/93-2a700443-cb03-4568-a5d1-857f9246ff84

Office of the Inspector General. "Revenue Investigations Director Terminated After OIG Investigation." *Georgia.gov*. March 15, 2020. Accessed August 10, 2025. https://oig.georgia.gov/press-releases/2020-03-15/revenue-investigations-director-terminated-after-oig-investigation

United States Attorney's Office Southern District of Georgia. "45 Defendants Charged On Gun, Drug Trafficking And Related Offenses Following Undercover Investigation." *Department of Justice*. June 19, 2013. Accessed August 10, 2025. https://www.justice.gov/usao-sdga/pr/45-defendants-charged-gun-drug-trafficking-and-related-offenses-following-undercover

WTOC. "US Attorney, ATF agent affair subject of investigation by Justice Department's Office of Inspector General." *WTOC 11 The Southeast News Leader*. March 3, 2015. Accessed August 10, 2025. https://www.wtoc.com/story/

28253788/us-attorney-atf-agent-affair-subject-of-investigation-by-justice-departments-office-of-inspector-general/

WTOC. "Ga. Department of Revenue agent arrested in illegal gambling investigation." *WTOC 11 The Southeast News Leader.* July 19, 2019. Accessed August 10, 2025. https://www.wtoc.com/2019/07/20/ga-department-revenue-agent-arrested-illegal-gambling-investigation/

ABOUT THE AUTHOR

Lou Valoze is a former undercover federal agent with the Bureau of Alcohol, Tobacco, Firearms, and Explosives (ATF), where he spent over twenty years infiltrating violent criminal organizations. Known for pioneering long-term undercover storefront operations, Valoze posed as a black-market arms dealer to dismantle some of the most dangerous gangs and gun traffickers in the country. His work led to hundreds of convictions and earned him national recognition for both bravery and innovation in law enforcement. He is the only agent in history to purchase more than one thousand crime guns in an undercover capacity. After retiring, Valoze began speaking publicly about the psychological toll of undercover work and the blurred lines between duty and identity. He is the author of *Storefront Sting*, a raw, unflinching memoir that offers an inside look at the risks, moral conflicts, and adrenaline-charged reality of life deep undercover. He is a graduate of Lafayette College in Easton, Pennsylvania.

Kerry Linfoot is a deputy sheriff and is assigned to a multi-jurisdictional investigative unit. She conducts multi-national narcotics investigations and has acted as the undercover officer for federal narcotics, firearms, and financial crimes cases. She completed her PhD in forensic linguistics at the University of Florida and, in her spare time, she teaches college-level writing classes and writes books. Originally from the United Kingdom, she currently lives in Colorado Springs, Colorado.